PRELUDE TO
ISRAEL

AN ANALYSIS OF ZIONIST DIPLOMACY, 1897-1947

by

ALAN R. TAYLOR

PHILOSOPHICAL LIBRARY
New York

CONTENTS

PREFACE

The object of this book is to analyze the nature of Zionism and to give a candid picture of the movement in operation, concentrating on the diplomatic activities of its leadership. It is to show the origin of a political movement, the formulation of its aim, and the implementation of policies designed to fulfill that aim. It is to examine the modern political phenomenon of Zionism in historical perspective and to demonstrate its unity of purpose and consistency of action. It is to throw light on the whole story of Zionist political activity, for it is a duty of the historian to bring clarity and completeness of narrative to his subject. His mission is to render a true picture of that subject, interpreting to show the relation between facts, but not to pass moral judgment. Today, the story of Zionist diplomacy is obscure, but the inevitable course of historical investigation will some day make it otherwise. It is to that task that this book is dedicated.

This book also has a secondary purpose. It seeks not only to engender a clearer concept of the nature and history of Zionism, but also to dispel certain misconceptions about the movement. For example, Zionism is frequently regarded as a religious movement. In actual fact, however, it is fundamentally secular, and its leaders have regarded it as such. Zionism is an answer to the secular problem of anti-Semitism. Its basic premise is that the only solution to this problem is the creation of a Jewish state and the attribution of national status to Jewish character. In a deeper sense, it is the reaction of East European Jewry to ghetto life in Russia, Poland and

v

Germany. It was here that the movement started, not in the West, where great strides in the assimilation of Jews have been made. In time, however, the movement spread, for the founders realized that they could not justify their premise without the support of world Jewry. In their search for the support of all Jews, the Zionists employed the romantic idea of the "return," a concept which holds emotional appeal for all Jews. It was thus that Zionism became mistakenly confused with Judaism, but this did not alter the essentially secular character of the Zionist movement.

A second misconception which this book seeks to set right concerns the manner in which Israel came to be. Many believe that the establishment of the state was an entirely spontaneous affair, arising out of the traditional longing of Jews to return to Palestine. Historical examination, however, reveals that the creation of Israel is the result of Zionist planning and organized effort. In the early years of this century, only a handful of world Jewry took any active interest in the Zionist idea, and it was not until the Second World War that even a majority of Jews became sympathetic with Zionism. It was Zionist activity which not only drew Jews into the movement, but also prepared the way for Jewish statehood through concrete action. It would not be fair to the past leaders of Zionism to deny their rightful claim to having made Israel with their own hands.

Throughout the book, reference is made to activities which were planned and carried out by the leaders of Zionism. It should be pointed out here that it is at times impossible to prove that such planning and direction took place by reference to minutes of top level Zionist meetings or documents published by Zionist leaders. However, it may be assumed that planning and direction existed, when all evidence points to coordinated action and the existence of policy direction. Similarly, it is not paradoxical that Zionism has remained unified and directed, though the movement has always been divided into factions. There is divergence of opinion within Zionism, but there also has always been a leadership which directs the movement toward the fulfillment of the aims which were clearly and firmly established at its inception.

One further remark concerning the nature of Zionism should be made to avoid confusion in the reader's mind. In the early years of the movement, there were two types of adherents: those seeking cultural as opposed to those seeking political fulfillment. The cultural Zionists were interested primarily in the rebirth of Hebraic culture, in the linguistic, religious, and ethnic connection of the Jews to historic Palestine. The political Zionists, on the other hand, were concerned with the Jewish problem, and to them, Palestine was the most logical place for the establishment of a Jewish national state. Some of the early political Zionists did not even insist on Palestine, a fact which demonstrates their far greater concern with the creation of Jewish nationality than with Jewish culture and the romantic notion of the "return." When Zionism was organized in the late nineteenth century, the political adherents gained control of the movement, and thus when the term "Zionism" is not further qualified in this book, it will refer to what should more accurately be called "political Zionism."

The author gratefully acknowledges the assistance of his sister-in-law, Phyllis Hoffman Taylor, who not only typed the manuscript, but also made many helpful editorial suggestions. The author also acknowledges the careful guidance and stylistic suggestions of Mr. Richard Norman Tetlie, founder of the United States Information Service in Israel. Mr. Tetlie's unremitting objectivity and intimate knowledge of the subject matter made him an invaluable mentor and a real contributor to the publication of this book. The assistance of Professor George E. Kirk of Harvard University, who made many corrections and suggestions, is gratefully acknowledged. The interpretation, however, is entirely that of the author. The portraits of leading Zionists were supplied by courtesy of Zionist Archives and Library of the Palestine Foundation Fund. Finally, the author expresses his appreciation for the painstaking efforts of his wife, Lydia Schurman Taylor, whose contribution to the preparation of the manuscript was above and beyond the call of duty.

Washington, D. C.   A. R. T.

CHAPTER I

THE CREATION OF ZIONIST AIMS AND POLICY

The Beginnings of Political Zionism

The idea of Zionism has existed for centuries as a facet of Jewish and Christian thought.[1] In the former, it has been the result of an association of Judaism with the ancient kingdom of the Hebrews in Palestine. In the latter, it has existed since the Cromwellian period, when it was supposed that the coming of the Millennium, or the thousand year reign of Christ on earth, would be accompanied by a restoration of the Jews to Palestine.

As a political movement, however, Zionism is a creation of the nineteenth century. The concern of the thinkers of the past one hundred and fifty years with sociology and religion, and the creation of model states led to the alleviation of the condition of the Jews in the Diaspora[2] and the development of the idea of the restoration. At first glance, it might seem that the improvement in the status of Jewry, climaxed by the recognition of its emancipation by Bismarck in 1871,[3] should have led to a solution of the Jewish Question in the Diaspora and an assimilation of Jews into the Gentile societies where they were born.

However, two barriers to this possibility began to emerge. Among the Jews themselves, there was a certain resistance to the evolution of a pattern which implied the loss of their identity as a people.[4] As Nahum Goldmann has phrased it,

1

"The object of the Jewish State has been the preservation of the Jewish people, which was imperilled by emancipation and assimilation. . . ." In Christendom, the gradual replacement of the religious fervor of the early part of the nineteenth century with racist nationalism in the latter decades led to resistance to the assimilation of Jewry.[5]

The incident which touched off the spark of Jewish separatism and Gentile anti-Semitism was the assassination of Tsar Alexander II of Russia in 1881. The Russian authorities made the Jews the scapegoat of the assassination and encouraged the precipitation of the infamous pogroms.[6] A mass exodus of Jews from Russia and the Pale of Settlement in Poland[7] followed on the heels of this outburst of anti-Semitism. Most of the refugees resettled in Western Europe and America, but some three thousand emigrated to Palestine.[8] In 1882, these emigres founded a colony near Jaffa called Rishon-le-Zion,[9] and the same year witnessed the establishment in Russia of a movement known as Chibbath Zion (Love of Zion).[10] The followers of Chibbath Zion organized themselves into societies—Choveve Zion (Lovers of Zion)[11]— and promoted the idea of a settlement in Palestine and the revival of the Hebrew language. The first seeds of political Zionism had taken root.

The Choveve Zion societies finally achieved official recognition in 1890 under the title of Society for Support of Jewish Agriculturalists and Artisans in Palestine and Syria.[12] This organization came under the leadership of Leon Pinsker, one of the founders of Chibbath Zion, and the first to forward the idea of a Jewish National Home, though not necessarily in Palestine.[13] Opposition to this nascent political Zionism was already apparent, however, both from within and without Jewish circles. Internally, a Jewish writer who employed the pen-name of Achad Ha'am came out in opposition to political Zionism, advocating instead a spiritual revival

2

which has come to be known as cultural Zionism.[14] Externally, the Ottoman Porte issued regulations in 1888 which forbade mass Jewish immigrations into Ottoman territory and restricted the entry of most foreign Jews into Palestine to three month pilgrimages.[15] This tended to thwart any serious colonization of Palestine by European Jews and to frustrate any hopes of the creation of a Jewish state, which never found strong backing except when proposed in connection with Palestine. The birth of organized political Zionism was thus arrested and awaited the advent of a capable midwife.

Herzl and the First Zionist Congress

The man who was to bring political Zionism into the world was Theodor Herzl, a Hungarian Jew educated in Vienna. Though trained in law, Herzl's talent in writing won him the position of Paris correspondent for the Vienna newspaper, *Neue Freie Presse,* in which position he was serving when the Dreyfus Affair of 1894 caught the attention of Europe. The implications of anti-Semitism in the Dreyfus case led Herzl to believe that the only answer to the Jewish Question was the creation of a Jewish state. He felt that if anti-Semitism could be aroused in liberal France, it was bound to appear with greater force in other countries. Therefore, in the summer of 1895 he composed a pamphlet entitled, *Der Judenstaat* (The Jewish State),[16] which advocated the establishment of British-sponsored Jewish colonization of Argentina or Palestine with a view to the eventual creation of a sovereign Jewish National State.

The fact that Herzl even considered Argentina as a prospective location for a Jewish state seems incongruous in the light of Zionism's later preoccupation with Palestine. However, it should be understood that Herzl's concern was a

3

solution to the problem of anti-Semitism, not the fulfillment of the prophesies of traditional Judaism.[17] Thus, political Zionism was, in its early stages, an essentially secular movement, and its basic character has always remained secular. The later allusion of the Zionists to the romantic idea of the "return" was injected into the movement largely because of its emotional appeal. But this does not alter the fact that political Zionism has always been a rational rather than an ideological movement. It has sought a specific solution to a specific problem, not the glorification of an ethno-religious ideal.

The publication of *Der Judenstaat* in 1896 provoked both favorable and antagonistic reactions in Gentile and Jewish circles alike. Herzl felt, however, that a sizable segment of Jewry was drawn to his idea, and he began pressing for the convention of a World Congress of Zionists, an idea originally suggested by the inventor of the term "Zionism," Nathan Birnbaum.[18] With the support of those who shared his views, Herzl succeeded in convening the First Zionist Congress at Basle in August, 1897. This Congress was to the Zionist movement what the Constitutional Convention was to the nascent United States. In the opening address Herzl outlined the purpose of the meeting: "We are here to lay the foundation stone of the house which is to shelter the Jewish nation."[19] The program he proposed included (1) the promotion of an organized, large scale Jewish colonization of Palestine, (2) the acquisition of an internationally recognized legal right to colonize Palestine, and (3) the formation of a permanent organization to unite all Jews in the cause of Zionism.[20]

This formula, though expressed in different terms and with varying specifications during the following sixty years, has remained the essential foundation of Zionist policy. The three problems that faced political Zionism before the State

4

of Israel was established were the actual entry of sufficient numbers of Jews into Palestine to make possible the formation of a *de facto* state, the question of support from Gentile nations, and the winning of the majority of Jews to the Zionist cause. It will also be noted that a revised form of this policy directed Zionism even after 1948.[21] At different points each one of these three policy aims received particular stress, but they remained equally important and mutually inter-dependent policy requirements. And though factions arose which emphasized one requirement over the others, Zionism remained consistent, united, and continuous, never lacking in clarity of purpose.

The Basle Congress terminated with the formulation of an official program. The ultimate goal was outlined in these words: "The aim of Zionism is to create for the Jewish people a home in Palestine secured by public law."[22] The steps to be taken in contemplation of the fulfillment of this aim were: (1) the promotion of Jewish colonization of Palestine, (2) the establishment of an organization to bind world Jewry by means of institutions in each country containing Jews, (3) the strengthening of Jewish national sentiment, and (4) the acquisition of government consent to the attainment of the aim of Zionism.[23]

The aim of Zionism, as stated in the official program of the Congress, was as Herzl conceived it, except for the fact that he contemplated a "state" rather than a "home." However, those who formulated the program, though they concurred with Herzl on this matter, realized that many Jews, indeed a majority at that time, objected to the idea of a Jewish nation, not to mention the objections of the Turkish Government. Thus, in accordance with the requirement of the Zionist program dealing with the problem of the backing of world Jewry, they deliberately used the word "Heimstatte" (homestead). This prevented the program from being offensive to non-political Zionists and at the same time implied the creation of an autonomous community, a concept which could easily be construed as implying statehood at a later date. Herzl himself remarked on this matter by saying, "No need to worry [about the phraseology]. The people will read it as 'Jewish State' anyhow."[24] The steps were also a repetition of those proposed by Herzl, with the minor exception that step three of Herzl's program was embodied in two steps, two and three, of the official program of the Congress.

The Basle Congress also brought into existence the World Zionist Organization, thus bringing to life the child, political Zionism, whose birth had been arrested and was awaiting the midwifery of Herzl. The Organization was to serve as the government proper of a pre-natal Israel. An Actions Committee was formed to deal with pressing issues while the Congress of the Organization was out of session, and an Inner Actions Committee, or Executive, was created to serve as a permanent leadership which would guide policy.[25] These Committees took on primarily the functions of a foreign office, since the aim of the Zionist Organization was foreign in character. Thus, in 1897, the aim and policies of political Zionism were established, and a governmental structure was brought into existence to seek attainment of the aim through implementation of the policies.

The Zionist Organization Prior to World War I

Herzl, who was elected the first President of the Zionist Organization, believed that the most important policy requirement of political Zionism was point two of his original formula—the acquisition of an internationally recognized legal right to colonize Palestine. Therefore, in October, 1898, he met with Kaiser Wilhelm II in Constantinople, where the German monarch had stopped on a tour through the

Near East.[26] Herzl proposed the creation of a Chartered Land Development Company, which would be operated by Zionists under German protectorate. A second meeting with the Kaiser took place in Palestine on November 2, 1898, but at this audience the Kaiser announced his opposition to the proposal, realizing that such a German-sponsored intervention in Ottoman affairs would give alarm to Great Britain, France, and Russia.[27]

Herzl's next move was to confront the Sultan of Turkey with his proposition for Jewish settlement in Palestine. This he did in May, 1901, approaching the subject indirectly with the suggestion that Jews could assist in the reorganization of the finances of the Porte and also in the development of the natural resources of the Ottoman Empire.[28] This enticing offer failed, however, to sway the Sultan, and he replied that he could not permit any mass immigration of Jews into Palestine.

Having failed to obtain legalization of Jewish colonization of Palestine from the Kaiser and the Sultan, Herzl concentrated his attention on England.[29] In October, 1902, the Executive entered into negotiations with the British Government, seeking to obtain a grant of portions of the Sinai Peninsula in which an autonomous Jewish settlement would be established.[30] The negotiations broke down owing to certain Egyptian stipulations, a first hint of the future Arab opposition to Zionism. In the following year, however, the British Government came forth with an offer, which had been prompted by Herzl, to turn over Uganda to the Zionist Organization for the purpose of colonization.[31] Even though Herzl backed the acceptance of the Uganda proposal as a temporary measure, the Sixth Zionist Congress did not propose any concrete action other than the sending of a commission to investigate Uganda.[32]

With the death of Herzl in 1904, Zionism split into two

factions. One supported Herzl's view that the main problem was that of international sanction and the establishment of an immediate solution to the Jewish Question, whether in Palestine or elsewhere. This group came to be known as the "politicals." The other faction, strongly influenced by the cultural revivalism of the Choveve Zion societies, refused to consider any proposal for the building up of a Jewish home or nation in any place other than Palestine. These were referred to as the "practicals." At the Seventh Zionist Congress in 1905, the "practicals" demonstrated a greater show of strength, and a resolution was passed in which it was declared that Zionism was concerned solely with Palestine.[33]

Unfortunately, the titles which were attached to the two factions that arose within political Zionism at the time of the Uganda proposal are misleading. Both groups were adherents of political Zionism, the only difference being that one accentuated legalization and the other stressed colonization of Palestine and an historico-cultural Romanticism. Eventually, the two trends—political realism and Romantic nationalism —were to join together and form one platform. Later, the third element of the program—the rallying of world Jewry to the cause—was to become a major Zionist concern in view of the fact that in 1914 only 130,000 of the thirteen million Jews in the world were Zionists.[34]

Thus, Herzl's tripartite program held together. From 1905 to 1914, colonization of Palestine continued gradually, and at the outbreak of World War I, fifty-nine Jewish colonies with some twelve thousand inhabitants existed in Palestine.[35] Also, a group of discerning Jews, who did not underrate the importance of political recognition, had moved to England in search of sympathetic backing.[36]

Arthur James Balfour

Dr. Theodor Herzl

Sir Herbert Samuel

(*Zionist Archives and Library of the Palestine Foundation Fund*)

Nahum Sokolov

Abba Hillel Silver

David Ben-Gurion

Stephen S. Wise

Chaim Weizmann

CHAPTER II

THE BALFOUR DECLARATION

Zionist Policy and World War I

The Zionist interest in England, which was initiated by
Herzl and developed during the decade following his death,[1]
became greatly intensified shortly after the outbreak of World
War I. With the involvement of Turkey, the future of Palestine became uncertain. The Zionists were quick to see that
what had been a frustrating search for unlimited immigration into Palestine and for the establishment of a recognized
and legalized Zionist political status could now be successful.
Immediately, England became the uppermost concern of the
Zionist Organization.

Chaim Weizmann, a Jewish chemist from Russia, had
moved to England in 1904 and was destined to become the
new leader of the Zionist movement. He had come there on
the conviction that the British were the most promising
potential sympathizers of Zionism, and in 1906 had embarked
on a program of establishing rapport with British politicians
in a meeting with Arthur Balfour.[2] Later, in reference to this
meeting, Balfour called Weizmann, "the man who made me
a Zionist."[3]

Furthermore, Weizmann, originally a member of the "practical" faction of the Zionist Organization, had been a champion of fusion of the factions within political Zionism.[4] The
deadlock between the "politicals" and the "practicals" had

9

been broken at the Eighth Congress in 1907,[5] and with the advent of the First World War, Weizmann's "organic" Zionism became predominant. The Herzlian three-point program —organization, recognition, and colonization—was brought back into focus, and the "synthesis," as it is sometimes called, was symbolized in the person of Dr. Weizmann. This re-emphasis of the original platform was a natural development arising out of the basic unity of Zionism and it was also a logical reassertion of the outlook of the "politicals" at a time when the status of Palestine seemed bound to change and a program of political action within Gentile nations was obviously needed.

Therefore, as the champion of fusion and the leading Zionist in England, Weizmann emerged as the most important single person in the Zionist Organization. It is also significant that Weizmann had a developed sense of the importance of Gentile support at this time when it was so vital to Zionism to win such support. Already in 1907, Weizmann showed his awareness of the importance of Gentile recognition of Zionism:

> Political Zionism means: to make the Jewish question an international one. It means going to the nations and saying to them: 'We need your help to achieve our aim. . . .'[6]

Once the decision was made to concentrate Zionist activity on winning England as Zionism's ally, Weizmann was joined by two of the leading Zionists on the Continent—Sokolow and Tschlenow.[7] Plans were made to concentrate on two endeavors: (1) the winning of British Jews to Zionism, a task which Weizmann had begun just before the war by interesting the Rothschilds in a project to found a university in Palestine,[8] and (2) the development of friends for Zionism among the top leaders in the British Government.

Weizmann's acquaintance with Balfour was of little use in

1914, since the latter was not a Cabinet member, and it was therefore necessary to cultivate new contacts. Of primary importance in this effort was a chance meeting in 1914 between Weizmann and C. P. Scott, then editor of the *Manchester Guardian*. Weizmann almost immediately won Scott to the cause of Zionism, and the latter introduced Weizmann, Sokolow, and Tschlenow to Lloyd George and Herbert Samuel, both members of the Cabinet.[9] Lloyd George and Samuel, the latter a Jew himself, showed sympathy, and thus began a period of Zionist diplomatic preparation designed to muster British support.

The conversion of Scott to the Zionist cause, just as that of Balfour, exemplifies the phenomenon of Gentile Zionism, which is at best only vaguely understood. Arnold Toynbee offers two explanations. First, he suggests that the pro-Zionist inclinations of some Gentiles may be derived from a sense of guilt arising out of a subconscious anti-Semitism.[10] He also attributes Gentile Zionism in Anglo-Saxon countries to a ". . . characteristically 'Anglo-Saxon' attitude of combining an unavowed yet patent Machiavellianism with a suspect yet sincere Quixotry. . . ."[11] Christopher Sykes offers Christian millenarianism as an explanation of Gentile Zionism in England.[12] Certainly many Christians have supported Zionism because they feel that biblical prophesy foretells the restoration of the Jews to Palestine. As one scholar has pointed out, however, the modern Jews have neither national nor covenant continuity with the Jews of biblical Israel, and even if they did it is very doubtful that scripture speaks of any "return" beyond that from Babylon.[13] Thus, if Christians have supported Zionism on religious grounds, what is most surprising is that they have inquired into the biblical justification for Zionism with so uncritical and so unsearching an eye.

Beyond these arguments, it may be further suggested that

11

the willingness of Gentiles to go out of their way to assist Zionism arises out of a confusion in their minds as to the relationship between Zionism and liberalism. In point of observation, many Gentiles have supported Zionism with the conviction that they are serving the cause of racial tolerance by so doing. In actual fact, however, it is the assimilationist Jews who have sought a liberal solution to racism, while the Zionists have sought a national solution. Yet the confusion in the minds of Gentiles has existed, and this serves partially to explain their pro-Zionist leanings.

The Diplomatic Groundwork in England

In November, 1914, just one month before his meeting with Samuel and Lloyd George, Dr. Weizmann outlined the Zionist position to be laid before the British Government. This was contained in a letter to Scott, which read:

> . . . we can reasonably say that should Palestine fall within the British sphere of influence, and should Britain encourage Jewish settlement there, as a British dependency, we could have in twenty to thirty years a million Jews out there, perhaps more; they would develop the country, bring back civilization to it and form a very effective guard for the Suez Canal.[14]

Here, then, was a crystallization of Zionism's war policy. In concise form, its goals were: (1) an Allied victory, (2) the establishment of a British mandate in Palestine, (3) an understanding that such a British mandatory would then facilitate the entry of a million or more Jews into Palestine within a period of twenty to thirty years after the mandate was established, and (4) an understanding that the mandate would terminate in a Jewish controlled Palestine which would continue to serve Britain's interest in the Suez Canal

12

by acting as a bulwark to the defense of that waterway. It is interesting to note that all four points have been fulfilled.

Following their meeting with the three Zionists, Lloyd George and Herbert Samuel began to assist Weizmann in his search to enlist the support of the British Government. Samuel, who was pro-Zionist before his meeting with Weizmann, had already broached the subject of the creation of a Jewish state in Palestine to Sir Edward Grey, the Foreign Secretary.[15] Grey had said that he would work for the realization of such a state in the future,[16] and thus had joined the ranks of the pro-Zionists in the British Government. In January, 1915, Samuel went a step further by issuing an official memorandum entitled, "The Future of Palestine."[17] In it he advocated the immigration of three to four million Jews into Palestine under British protection.

The pro-Zionist case had been stated and immediately faced its first trial run in search of Cabinet support. It was doomed to failure this time, however, by the opposition of the Prime Minister, Herbert Asquith, who was committed to a policy of replacing the Turks with the Arabs as friends of Great Britain in the Near East.[18] At the same time, the leaders of assimilated British Jewry informed the Zionists that they did not favor the establishment of a Jewish home as the answer to the Jewish Question, that they felt Zionism's national postulate would only promote anti-Semitism, and that they could not open discussions with a Zionist Organization which contained members in enemy countries.[19]

To offset the influence of non-Zionist British Jewry, the Zionists embarked upon an extensive propaganda campaign designed to win supporters among British Jews and non-Jews, and to create the impression that the majority of world Jewry backed the Zionist cause. Herbert Sidebotham,[20] a prominent English journalist associated with the *Manchester Guardian* and a pro-Zionist, organized the British Palestine Committee to spread Zionist ideas throughout the United Kingdom.[21] Other pro-Zionist writers, notable among whom was Norman Bentwich, joined the campaign to popularize the Zionist cause and develop backing for it.[22] In one of his editorials, Sidebotham reflected the view of Kitchener that Palestine should become a bulwark of British defense of the Suez Canal,[23] thus playing up the strategic value to Britain of a friendly and dependable Jewish state in Palestine. This argument carried great weight and brought many into sympathy with Zionist aims. It is interesting to note, however, that the unreliability of Zionism as a strategic ally for Britain was demonstrated in later years.

The propaganda campaign of 1915 and 1916 was paralleled by a continuing attempt to gather sufficient support for Zionism in the British Government to precipitate an official British policy committed to the Zionist cause. At the suggestion of Lloyd George, Weizmann renewed his contact with Balfour. The latter announced his complete sympathy and asked what he might do to help.[24] At the time, Weizmann's conversion of Balfour did not seem particularly important, but when Balfour was appointed to the Cabinet in May, 1915, he assumed the status of another major recruit for Zionism. Gradually, a trend towards at least partial recognition of Zionist aims began to unfold.

The first step in the second attempt of the Zionists to win the British Government to their cause was to get Dr. Weizmann stationed in London where he could be in close contact with Government officials. In his first meeting with Lloyd George, Chairman of the War Munitions Committee, Weizmann had learned that the British Government was in need of a method to produce acetone for explosives in large quantities.[25] During 1915, Weizmann developed just such a method and informed Scott of his success. Scott made several trips to London to urge Lloyd George, Balfour, and others to make use of Weizmann.[26] Finally, in December, 1915, Scott took Weizmann to see Lloyd George, and in February, 1916, Weizmann was appointed to the Admiralty under the supervision of Balfour.[27] Weizmann studiously avoided the question of Zionism, but Balfour, remembering his earlier promise, announced to Weizmann one day, "You know after the war you may get your Jerusalem."[28]

It was at this point, early in 1916, that the British Government began actively to consider a more favorable official attitude toward Zionism. The pro-Zionist members of the Cabinet moved cautiously, realizing the position of Asquith, and contented themselves with an immediate goal of sounding out France, Russia, and the United States. In March, 1915, Sir Edward Grey sent a memorandum outlining British thoughts on the relationship between Palestine and world Jewry to Sir Edward Buchanan, the British ambassador in St. Petersburg.[29] This memorandum, which Buchanan was instructed to pass on to the Russian Minister of Foreign Affairs, M. Sazanoff, stated that the British Government was anxious to devise some means of gaining the support of a majority of the Jews in the world for the Allied cause. It went on to express the belief that if Jewish colonists in Palestine could compete with the Arab population, then the administration of the country might be placed in Jewish hands. It was proposed that some agreement be reached which would envision such a program, the idea being that the agreement would serve to draw world Jewry to the Allied cause. The Russians expressed their support of the proposal, but insisted that Russian religious interests in the Holy Land be safeguarded.

The story of the continuation of this plan on Britain's part to reach an agreement with her allies on the question of Zionism during the year of 1916 is largely the story of Mark Sykes. In the autumn of 1915, Sykes had been appointed as

Assistant Secretary to the War Cabinet. There were only two such positions, and the fact that Sykes was given charge primarily of Near Eastern affairs made him a very important person in the eyes of Zionist recruiters. Sometime before 1914, a British Zionist named Moses Gaster had exposed Sykes to the principles of Zionism, and, according to Sykes himself, it was Gaster who converted him to the cause shortly after his appointment to the service of the War Cabinet.[30]

Just after the presentation of Grey's memorandum to Sazanoff, Sykes arrived in St. Petersburg to open the discussions which led to the famous Sykes-Picot Agreement, contracted between France, Great Britain, and Russia. Approaching Sazanoff first, Sykes suggested that Zionism might prove the solution to the Jewish problem within Russia.[31] At the same time, Sykes was responsible for preventing the communication to the French Government of a memorandum warning of the dangers of Jewish nationalism sent to the British Government by Lucien Wolf, a British anti-Zionist Jew.[32] This action incurred Sykes an official rebuke.

Turning next to the French, Sykes persuaded M. Georges-Picot, the French negotiator of the Sykes-Picot Agreement, that it was vital to attach American Jewry to the Allied cause as a means of getting America into the war. He then convinced Georges-Picot that only by promising that after the war the Holy Land would be placed under an administration favorable to Zionism could American Jewry be drawn to the Allied cause.[33] Subsequently, the French Government sent a Jewish professor, Victor Guillaume Basch, to the United States to assure American Jewry that the Jewish colonies in Palestine would be afforded the full protection of Britain and France after the conclusion of the war.[34] The Basch mission failed to arouse much enthusiasm among American Jews, and Sykes began to lose interest in Zionism as a means

16

of getting America into the war, a development which he considered vital.

The Sykes-Picot Agreement was, in a sense, contrary to the desires of the Zionists in that it provided for an international control of Palestine instead of a mandate run by a pro-Zionist British Government. On the other hand, however, it served to negate any implied promises to the Arabs, thus eliminating the possibility of Arab control and affording the Zionists time to wrest Palestine for themselves. In this sense, it served the Zionist cause, though it is almost certain that the Zionists did not promote the Agreement themselves. They continued to concentrate on the conversion of British officials to their cause in the hope of eventually obtaining an official backing from the British Government, a policy which seldom failed to bring the results they desired.

In October of 1916, Sykes was approached by a pro-Zionist Armenian, one James Malcolm, probably, though not certainly at the instigation of the Zionist Organization. Malcolm succeeded in reviving Sykes' sympathy for Zionism, stressing the fact that Justice Brandeis, a prominent American Zionist, had a special influence with President Wilson and could serve to help bring the United States into the war.[35] Won over by the argument, Sykes petitioned the Cabinet on several occasions to enter into direct negotiations with the Zionists. This the Cabinet finally agreed to do, but without any previous commitments. Malcolm was appointed as the go-between, and the Zionists prepared for action in the face of this climactic success.

Their first request was to be granted permission to use British communications facilities to contact Zionists throughout the world. The Cabinet granted the request, thus unwittingly establishing a precedent of cooperation with the Zionists and making it impossible to reverse this policy, owing to the fact that the communications facilities were used to proclaim British support of Zionism throughout world Jewry.[36] To withhold support once the seemingly insignificant request had been granted would have been to incur the wrath of Zionist Jews the world over.

At this momentous point in the history of political Zionism, a draft of Zionist proposals to be used as a basis of negotiation with the British Government was drawn up. This document, which was presented to the British Government, was entitled "Programme for a New Administration of Palestine in Accordance with the Aspirations of the Zionist Movement."[37] It proposed the establishment of a semi-governmental Jewish company in Palestine under the suzerainty of Britain or France. The company was to have a national status and was so allowed to encourage Jewish colonization of Palestine. The Zionist case rested on this proposal until December, 1916, when Lloyd George replaced Asquith as Prime Minister and became leader of the Second Coalition Government. Lloyd George, as has been noted, had been recruited to the Zionist cause, and thus the battle was really over. With the Prime Minister in the Zionist camp and the appointment of Balfour, another pro-Zionist, to the headship of the Foreign Office, a British commitment to Zionism was assured. It was only a matter of time.

The Preparation of the Balfour Declaration

In February, 1917, less than two months after the formation of the Second Coalition Cabinet, Mark Sykes was assigned to open official negotiations with the Zionists. The first meeting,[38] which was dedicated to an airing of views, was held at the home of Moses Gaster, a setting which undoubtedly reminded Sykes of his earliest talks with Gaster and his ultimate conversion to Zionism. Gaster opened the meeting with a statement to the effect that Zionism envisioned the fulfill-

18

ment of its aim through the medium of British suzerainty alone. This served to reassure the British Government that its own strategic interests in Palestine would receive consideration as an integral part of any agreement reached between itself and the Zionist Organization. Thus, the Zionists began their talks by implying the establishment of a deal and by providing the British with a sense of justification in what they were doing.[39]

Herbert Samuel followed Gaster, expressing the hope that the Jews of Palestine would receive a fully national status, and that Jews in the Diaspora would be considered as sharing in this national status. The impossible nature of the latter suggestion in the light of the prevalent concept of the obligations of a citizen to his national state seems to have escaped Samuel completely.

Weizmann rose next and stated that the mandatory of Palestine should embark on its administration with the understanding that nothing would be done to restrict Jewish immigration in any manner. He, in turn, was followed by Mr. Harry Sacher, who reiterated Samuel's proposals by saying that Jews outside of Palestine should be allowed to share in Jewish nationality. He added that such an extension of Jewish nationality beyond the borders of Palestine shouldn't involve the usual political implications of citizenship. Like Samuel, Sacher preferred to gloss over the inevitable dilemma in the matter of political allegiance implied by the creation of a Jewish nationality, a problem which lives with every non-Israeli Jew in the world today.

At the same meeting, Sykes, undoubtedly moved by the need for more realistic considerations, noted that certain problems stood in the way of the Zionist proposals.[40] These included the skepticism of Russia, the impending opposition of the Arabs, and the French insistence on the creation of a French mandate in all of Syria, including Palestine.

The Zionists ended the meeting by summarizing their fundamental desires:[41] (1) an internationally recognized right of the Jews to Palestine, (2) the establishment of juridical nationhood for the Jewish community in Palestine, (3) a chartered Jewish company to be created in Palestine with rights to acquire land, (4) the union of Palestine under one administration, and (5) the establishment of extraterritoriality in the holy places of Palestine. The first three of these points embody the Zionist aims, while the latter two were designed to placate England and Russia, respectively.

With the inclusion of elements in the proposal designed to stimulate the favor of England and Russia, only France and the Arabs remained as interested but uncommitted partners. Though the population of Palestine was composed predominantly of Arabs, the Zionists had never taken them into consideration, and did not even mention them in the many Congresses starting with the first in 1897.[42] Thus, Weizmann and the other Zionists in England at the time of the negotiations leading to the Balfour Declaration concerned themselves primarily with bringing France into support of their proposals, giving secondary consideration to the development of a friendly attitude in the United States and Italy.

Mark Sykes was the first to see the importance to the Zionists of obtaining French approval. On February 8, 1917, he put Sokolow in touch with M. Georges-Picot at the French Embassy in London.[43] Sokolow informed Georges-Picot that the Zionists considered it imperative to their interests that the mandate for Palestine be granted to Great Britain. He succeeded in winning Georges-Picot to the Zionist point of view, but still to be faced was the problem of obtaining the official support of the French Government, which was strongly under the influence of a group intent on the establishment of French suzerainty in all Syria. This group was known as the "Syrian Party." Sokolow, however, was not discouraged. He had begun the recruitment of the French Government by winning Georges-Picot, and he had only to continue this process in France to bring the same favorable results as it had already brought in England. Joined by Sykes and Malcolm, he proceeded to Paris in March, 1917. Sykes put Sokolow in touch with the proper French authorities and then used his connections to investigate the thinking of the "Syrian Party" and to facilitate Sokolow's mission.[44]

While Sokolow was putting the Zionist platform before the French Government, Sykes proceeded to Italy, where he paved the way for a favorable reception for Sokolow in the Italian Government and at the Vatican.[45] Thus, when Sokolow arrived in Rome, he was greeted with open arms, though it was with some difficulty that he dispelled the Pope's concern for the fate of the non-Jewish communities in Palestine.[46]

On his return to Paris, he was presented with an official letter from Jules Cambon, the Secretary-General to the French Foreign Ministry.[47] The letter expressed the sympathy of the French Government for the Zionist cause, and thus the mission of Sokolow was accomplished. The transfer of the support of the French Government from the "Syrian Party" to the Zionists was due not only to the work of Sykes, but also to the influence of Baron Edmond de Rothschild.[48] At the crucial moment this convert of Weizmann talked the anti-Zionist Alliance Israelite Universelle into backing the Zionist cause before the French Government, thus providing the needed extra weight to carry the day for Sokolow.

While Sokolow was on the Continent, the Zionists in England were busy preparing the draft of a resolution to be presented to the British Government as the basis of an official British statement on Zionism, while last minute efforts were made to insure British acceptance of the draft. Justice Brandeis assured Balfour that President Wilson looked with favor upon Zionism, while Weizmann tried to alleviate Balfour's

21

fears that Britain's allies would not accept a pro-Zionist policy on the part of Britain. Finally, on May 20, 1917, Weizmann announced before the English Zionist Federation that the British Government was prepared to announce its support of the aims of Zionism.[49]

Only a few days later, the anti-Zionist forces in British Jewry came out in opposition to political Zionism in a letter published in the *Times* written by two leading British Jews —David Alexander and Claude Montefiore.[50] Weizmann, alarmed that Balfour would lose heart, wrote a reassuring letter to the latter's secretary, in which he said, "The second category of British Jews [the Assimilationists] will fall into line quickly enough when this declaration [the Balfour Declaration] is given to us."[51] Weizmann had little reason to fear, however, since by announcing publicly that the British Government was committed to support Zionism, he had, in effect, closed the door behind the British Government and made it impossible to turn back on the course it had been following.

In June, Balfour announced his readiness to receive a draft of Zionist proposals to be embodied in an official statement of the British Government in support of Zionism. By July, the Zionists had arrived at a completed formula, which was duly presented to Balfour on the 18th of that month.[52] The formula proposed that the British Government announce its acceptance of the principle that Palestine be recognized as the National Home of the Jewish people, and that the Jews be granted the right to build up their national life in Palestine under conditions of internal autonomy and with the privilege of unconditional colonization. The Cabinet accepted the principle that Palestine be recognized as the National Home of the Jewish people, but insisted that means and methods be worked out by the British Government and the Zionist Organization.[53] The leading assimilationist British

Jews protested both the first and second formulas to the Cabinet, and it was at their insistence that the final formula, known as the Balfour Declaration,[54] called for the following: (1) British support of the establishment of a National Home for the Jews in Palestine, (2) British cooperation in the achievement of this objective, and (3) an understanding that nothing shall be done to prejudice the rights of existing non-Jewish communities in Palestine or the rights and status enjoyed by Jews in any other country.[55]

This was less than the Zionists had hoped for, since they envisioned the creation of a Palestine which would be "as Jewish as England is English." Such a Palestine could not be established in the light of the restrictions embodied in the Balfour Declaration. Nevertheless, they had to compromise, since a declaration of some sort which expressed favor of Zionism was vitally needed before the war ended. Also, they succeeded in getting Lloyd George to state that ". . . when the time arrived for according representative institutions to Palestine, if the Jews . . . had become a definite majority of the inhabitants, then Palestine would thus become a Jewish Commonwealth. . . ."[56] Thus, a way out was provided for the Zionists. They had only then to insure that the Jews became a majority in Palestine.

The Balfour Declaration ended the initial half of the first phase of Zionist policy. The Zionists had succeeded in establishing firmly the requirement of Herzl's program which called for the support of Gentile nations in establishing the legal right of the Jews to build a National Home in Palestine. The Balfour Declaration was not the result simply of British design to establish a buffer to the Suez Canal and to win the support of world Jewry to the Allied cause. More accurately, the coincidence of British and Zionist interests was employed by the Zionists to engender British support. Thus, the Balfour Declaration was the outcome of planned

Zionist diplomacy. A British official who came into contact with Weizmann summarizes this diplomatic victory in the following words:

> One of the best examples of . . . successful diplomacy is that by which Dr. Weizmann brought into existence the Jewish National Home . . . When [the first World War] began, his cause was hardly known to the principal statesmen of the victors. It had many enemies, and some of the most formidable were amongst the most highly placed of his own people. The task which Dr. Weizmann set himself of transferring the centre of Zionism to London and obtaining the co-operation of Britain in Palestine was more difficult than that of any other statesman of the smaller Powers . . . He once told me that 2,000 interviews had gone to the making of the Balfour Declaration. With unerring skill he adapted his arguments to the special circumstances of each statesman. To the British and Americans he could use biblical language and awake a deep emotional undertone; to other nationalities he more often talked in terms of interest. Mr. Lloyd George was told that Palestine was a little mountainous country not unlike Wales; with Lord Balfour the philosophical background of Zionism could be surveyed; for Lord Cecil the problem was placed in the setting of a new world organisation; while to Lord Milner the extension of imperial power could be vividly portrayed. To me, who dealt with these matters as a junior officer of the General Staff, he brought from many sources all the evidence that could be obtained of the importance of a Jewish National Home to the strategical position of the British Empire,[57] but he always indicated by a hundred shades and inflections of the voice that he believed that I could also appreciate better than my superiors other more subtle and recondite arguments.
>
> This skilful presentation of facts would, however, have been useless unless he had convinced all with whom he came into contact of the probity of his conduct and the reality of his trust in the will and strength of Britain.

Once the British Government had come out in favor of the recognition of the aim of Zionism, it remained to recruit the support of world Jewry and to colonize the field. The former, as Weizmann pointed out, would be taken care of in the course of time. The latter became the next immediate concern of the Zionists, and to that their attention next turned.

CHAPTER III

THE MANDATE

The Zionists at the Peace Conference

By the end of 1918, Zionist efforts had succeeded in precipitating official acceptance of the Balfour Declaration in France, Italy, the United States, and Japan.[1] Then, in January, 1919, the Peace Conference formally convened in Paris. On the 27th of the following month a Zionist delegation, representing the Zionist Organization, presented the Zionist case before the Supreme Council. Various members of the delegation, including Weizmann and Sokolow, addressed the Council on the several aspects of the draft resolutions which were contained in an official memorandum sent to the Supreme Council on February 3rd.[2] These resolutions called for: (1) the recognition of the historic title of the Jews to Palestine and the right of Jews to reconstitute their National Home in Palestine, (2) the establishment of certain boundaries for Palestine, designed to include southern Lebanon, Mount Hermon, Aqaba, and Transjordan, (3) the establishment of a mandate for Palestine under the administration of Great Britain, (4) the eventual realization of the Balfour Declaration, (5) the promotion of Jewish colonization of Palestine, and (6) the creation of a council representative of the Jews of Palestine. In effect, the Zionists were following up their attainment of a promise of British support with a formula specifying the way in which that promise should be carried out.[3]

The first action taken by the Peace Conference in regard to Palestine was the provision, contained in Article 22 of the Covenant of the League,[4] calling for the establishment of temporary mandates in "certain communities formerly belonging to the Turkish Empire."

Just one month before the adoption of the Covenant of the League by the Conference, the British delegation opened formal discussions with the Zionists on the matter of drafting what was to be the official mandate for Palestine. In a letter to David Hunter Miller[5] dated Paris, March 28, 1919, Felix Frankfurter outlined the basic points which the Zionists wished to have embodied in the text of the mandate.[6] It was proposed that: (1) the Balfour Declaration be restated in the text of the mandate, (2) the establishment in Palestine of a Jewish National Home to be developed into an autonomous commonwealth should be the guiding principle of the mandate, and (3) when the people of Palestine became ready for autonomy, a representative government would be established.

These proposals were subsequently revised and presented on July 15, 1919, to the British delegation as a draft to be considered for inclusion in the proposed treaty with Turkey.[7] This draft called for: (1) the ultimate aim of the mandate should be the creation in Palestine of a self-governing commonwealth, (2) the formation of a permanent Jewish council in Palestine, (3) sponsorship of the principle of a Jewish National Home, (4) facilitation of Jewish immigration and colonization, and (5) the establishment of Hebrew as the official language in Palestine. A third revision in August, 1919, went a step further by suggesting that the proposed Jewish National Home should comprise all of Palestine.[8]

In essence, the Zionist proposals asked that the Mandate for Palestine be dedicated to the creation of a Jewish state. The mandatory administration was to be devoted to the strengthening of the Jewish element in Palestine and was to continue in control of the country until such time as there were sufficient Jews in Palestine to make possible the establishment of a *de facto* Jewish state.

The British Government was disposed to accept the Zionist proposals, and on April 25, 1920, the Supreme Council, which was sitting at San Remo, assigned the mandate for Palestine to Great Britain. The text of the Treaty of Sèvres with Turkey, which was signed the following August, underwrote the Balfour Declaration,[9] and thus all that remained to insure the fulfillment of the aim of Zionism was the adoption of a mandate text which upheld the basic program of the Zionist proposals.

The appointment of Lord Curzon as Foreign Secretary in the spring of 1920 posed problems for the Zionists. Curzon had never been an ardent supporter of Zionism and was furthermore concerned over the growing tide of Arab opposition. He consequently insisted on omitting from the text of the mandate several Zionist-sponsored clauses, including one proclaiming the historical connection of the Jews with Palestine and another calling for the eventual establishment of a self-governing commonwealth in Palestine.[10] The Zionists exerted their influence on the Government through Balfour, Milner,[11] and Samuel, but were only successful in having retained the clause concerning the historical connection of the Jews with Palestine.[12]

Yet, as in the case of the Balfour Declaration, the Zionists were willing to compromise in the light of the sympathetic attitude of leading Government officials with the Zionist cause. When Weizmann had announced the support of the British Government for Zionism in the spring of 1917, he had told the English Zionist Federation that the aim of Zionism would be realized by stages, and that the first stage would have to be one of British control of Palestine.[13] Thus, even though the draft mandate which Balfour finally presented to the League Council for approval in December, 1920, was not exactly what the Zionists wanted, the final document issued in 1922 represented a Zionist victory.[14] The connection of the Jews with Palestine was recognized, the Balfour Declaration was underwritten, the Jews of Palestine were allowed the right of developing self-governing institutions, the mandatory committed itself to the facilitation of Jewish immigration, and provisions were made for the establishment of a Jewish Agency to assist the administration. This was all the Zionists really needed and the future was assured. As Temperley expresses it, "In effect, the Mandate grants to Zionism nearly all that the Zionist representatives asked for at the Paris Conference in 1919."[15] The first phase of the policy of political Zionism had ended in a resounding victory for the protagonists.

Zionist Representation in Palestine

In 1918, the British Government decided to send a Zionist Commission to Palestine to investigate means for the implementation of the Balfour Declaration.[16] The Commission was composed of Dr. Weizmann, Levi Bianchini of Italy, and Sylvain Levi, a non-Zionist French Jew who had been chosen by Edmond de Rothschild so that the Commission would not appear "packed" by Zionists. Once in the field, the Commission took over the work of the Palestine Office, which had been organized to represent the Zionist Organization in Palestine early in 1908. The Palestine Office was retained for a short period, but was finally absorbed by the Zionist Commission in October, 1919.[17] The primary political function of the Zionist Commission was to serve as a link between the Jewish community in Palestine and the British authorities,[18] and was thus of paramount importance as a parallel in the field to the liaison arrangement between the British and the Zionists in London. The Commission, which operated under the same privileged conditions in Palestine as the Zionist Organization had in Great Britain,[19] was enlarged by the Zionist Organization in 1919, and six leading Zionists were sent out to buttress Zionist interests in the field.[20] In 1921, the name of the Commission was changed to the Zionist Executive in Palestine.

Thus, in the light of the increasing importance of the requirement of Herzl's program dealing with the physical occupation of the field, the Zionists were preparing the way for the successful outcome of the second phase of the policy of political Zionism. The "political" battle had been won, and it was time to turn to the "practical" battle. The latter struggle was also to be based on the acquisition of a favored position with the British authorities, and it was of no small significance to the Zionists that Herbert Samuel was appointed the first High Commissioner for Palestine, even though he later turned out to be a partial disappointment in Zionist eyes.[21] Remarking on this appointment a year later, Dr. Weizmann disclosed:[22]

> I was mainly responsible for the appointment of Sir Herbert Samuel to Palestine. Sir Herbert Samuel is our friend. At our request he accepted that difficult position. We put him in that position. He is our Samuel.

The Arab Peoples

Throughout the history of political Zionism there has loomed in the background a shadow of impending danger to the aim of the Zionist movement. This shadow is that of the Arabs, the family to which the overwhelming majority of the population of Palestine belonged until the advent of the fulfillment of the aim of Zionism. Perhaps the Zionists realized that the fulfillment of their aim inevitably implied the displacement of the Arab population, and therefore studiously avoided coming face to face with this problem.[23] If so, their failure to heed Arab opposition was accompanied with warnings of trouble ahead. Thus, the Zionists overlooked a problem which stood as the greatest threat to the Jewish future in Palestine.

At the very inception of political Zionism, warnings came from within the movement itself against the dangers of building up the Jewish State at the expense of other peoples. One of Herzl's primary reasons for stressing the importance of sanction before colonization was his fear that a system of expropriation would only bring antagonistic forces into play against Zionism.[24] At the same time, in 1897, Achad Ha'am, the leader of cultural Zionism, warned against any premeditated or uncharitable exclusion by Zionists of the interests of the Arabs.[25] Ten years later, Isaac Epstein embodied these concerns about the Arabs in a proposal for positive action in the matter. He said, ". . . Zionists must reach an alliance with the Arabs. . . ."[26] These suggestions fell on deaf ears. The Zionists eliminated consideration of the Arabs from their thoughts and listened with sympathy to such men as Zangwill, who said, "Give the country without a people to the people without a country."[27]

The first sign of Arab objections to Zionism appeared with the Egyptian opposition to the project for a Jewish settlement in the Sinai Peninsula, which has already been mentioned.[28] The second sign was the protest of the Arab deputies in the Turkish Parliament in 1912 to the acquisition of a large area of land in Palestine by Jews.[29] The Young Turk Government, which had toyed with the idea of coming to an agreement with the Zionists, underwrote the Arab position, and thus the threat of Zionism was removed until the Balfour Declaration was issued.

Following the proclamation of the Balfour Declaration, Achad Ha'am correctly pointed out that, "If you build your house . . . in a place where there are other inhabited houses, you are sole master only so far as your front gate . . . . beyond the gate all the inhabitants are partners. . . ." [30] However, the majority of the Zionists failed to give consideration to such reflections, and continued to seek ". . . those rights and privileges in Palestine which shall enable the Jews to make it as Jewish as England is English. . . ." [31]

The Arabs reacted to the announcement of the Balfour Declaration with consternation. The British, anxious to maintain the friendly relations they had developed with the Arabs during the war, entered upon what was to become a long series of reassurances to the Arabs. Early in 1918, Hogarth put the Sherif of Mecca [32] at ease by stating that "Jewish settlement in Palestine would only be allowed in so far as would be consistent with the political and economic freedom of the Arab population." [33] The Sherif, in turn, welcomed the Jews to the Arab lands on the understanding that a Jewish state in Palestine would not be in the offing. [34]

Weizmann moved next to reassure the Arabs, and in early 1919 concluded an agreement with Feisal [35] which proclaimed Arab-Jewish friendship. [36] This compact was entered into by Emir Feisal on the basis of the understanding that the Arabs would be granted independence and the right of self-determination, as promised the previous year in the Declaration to the Seven and the Anglo-French Declaration. [37] It is reported that Feisal also wrote a letter expressing strong support for Zionism to Felix Frankfurter, a leading American Zionist. However, when the issue came up years later, Feisal said he did not remember having written such a letter and the Zionists were unable to produce the original document.[38]

Regardless of what Feisal's position on Zionism might have been, however, the fact remains that the great majority of the Arabs viewed Zionism with distrust. Furthermore, Feisal himself was confused and ill-equipped during the many negotiations in which he was involved just after the war,[39] and it seems apparent that he did not grasp the full significance of all that was taking place.

Once the Zionists actually began to exert their influence in Palestine, the Arabs reacted with a violent and united opposition. In April, 1920, the traditionally friendly relations between the Arabs and Jews of Palestine gave way to Arab hatred and rioting in Jerusalem.[40] In May of 1921 riots developed in Jerusalem, and a Palestinian Arab Congress issued a note of formal protest against the Balfour Declaration.[41]

Though the British continued in their attempt to reassure the Arabs, the fact remained that ". . . in issuing the Balfour Declaration and subsequently undertaking a mandate for Palestine in which its terms were embodied, Great Britain was condemning one or other of the two communities concerned to suffer a fearful catastrophe. . . ."[42] Thus, the reassurance of Winston Churchill in 1922 that the British Government did not aim to create a wholly Jewish Palestine,[43] did little to put the Arabs at ease. The Arabs did not know the circumstances under which the Zionists had in the truest sense recruited the British Government to serve their aims, but they did know that they were faced with the reality of being displaced and disenfranchised by a Zionism that was already upon them.[44] Their anxiety proved in time to be justified, for during the period of the Mandate some 300,000 Jewish immigrants were introduced into Palestine to compete with the Arabs and wrest Palestine for the Zionist Organization. And, in the words of a great British historian, it is incontestable that this was done ". . . .by the might of England against the will of the people. . . ."[45] He might have added that in actuality it was for the support of that might that the Zionist diplomats in Britain had worked since 1914. They gained it by winning the men upon whom it rested. This was their plan and this was their victory.

Ratification of the Mandate

In 1921, the Zionists found themselves confronted with obstacles to the ratification of the draft Mandate agreed upon by the British Cabinet and the Zionist Organization. In May, riots between Arabs and Jews broke out in Jaffa, and the question of Zionist rights and aspirations became a matter of international controversy. After the riots, an Arab delegation, headed by Musa Kazim Pasha, arrived in London and presented its grievances to British Members of Parliament and to the Colonial Office.[46]

By this time, the draft Mandate which had been presented to the League Council in December, 1920, had undergone two changes.[47] The clause of the Balfour Declaration concerning the civil and religious rights of existing non-Jewish communities in Palestine was inserted in the preamble of the new draft, whereas it had only appeared in one of the articles of the 1920 draft. This change was of no great importance, but it did show a general concern over the potential threat of Zionism to the rights of the Arabs of Palestine.

The second change was far more significant. A new article was inserted specifying that the Balfour Declaration could not apply to the territories east of the Jordan. This restriction, which was included so as to allow Great Britain to offer Transjordan to 'Abdullah as an emirate, was a serious whittling down of the original Zionist aspiration, which was the creation of the Jewish State in a Palestine which was to include Transjordan.

It was partly because of these setbacks and partly to raise money that Weizmann decided to make a tour of European capitals.[48] He traveled first to Rome, where he entered into conversations with representatives of the Vatican and of the Italian Government. In his talks with the former he gave reassurance that Zionism was not concerned with the Christian Holy Places in Palestine and with the latter he sought to allay fears that the Mandate for Palestine would become simply a cloak for the establishment of a British outpost in the Mediterranean.[49] In both cases, he attempted to disassociate Zionism from the British, who were regarded as a possible source of danger to the interests of the Vatican and the Italian Government.

Weizmann moved next to Berlin to raise money and then to Paris, both to raise funds and to have discussions with French officials. He talked with M. de Monzie and General Gouraud, bringing up with the latter the question of the northern frontiers of Palestine.[50] At this time the French were continuing to assert their right to become the mandatory of all Syria, and did not want to give their approval to the Palestine Mandate before the question of the French mandatory in Syria had reached a final solution.[51] Therefore, Weizmann made little headway with General Gouraud, who resented the separation of Palestine from the rest of Syria and felt that the whole business of a Mandate for Palestine was only a cover for the expansion of British influence in the Levant.[52] Weizmann's primary concern, of course, was to convince the French that the waters of the Litani were of vital importance to Palestine and should be included in the Mandate for that area.[53] Just as the original Zionist claim included Transjordan, it also included what is now southern

Lebanon.[54] However, Weizmann had no success with General Gouraud, and eventually the waters of the Litani became included within the area of the French Mandate.

While Weizmann was in Europe trying to prevent any further alteration in the draft Mandate of 1920 and to counter the influence of the Arab delegation on political circles in London, the Zionist Executive in the British capital was engaging in extensive correspondence and discussions with the Colonial Office in an attempt to prevent any further changes in the draft of the Mandate.[55] Meanwhile, opposition to Zionism was spreading in Great Britain. The Report of the Haycraft Commission, which had investigated the May riots at Jaffa, attributed the outburst of violence to Arab grievances in connection with the Zionist program, British favoritism toward the Jews, the disproportionate number of Jews in public service, and the over-extension of the authority of the Zionist Commission.[56] The Report also criticized Dr. Eder, head of the Zionist Commission, for suggesting that only Jews be allowed to bear arms, and attacked the Zionists for refusing to recognize the existence of traditions of nationality among the Arabs.

This rather derogatory critique of Zionism as it operated in Palestine stimulated an already inaugurated trend against Zionism in Great Britain. A number of British newspapers began a campaign against Zionism, and in the House of Lords a motion introduced by Lord Islington and others calling for the repeal of the Balfour Declaration was passed.[57] By this time, Weizmann had returned to London, and his first task was to attempt to prevent the House of Commons from passing a similar motion. Weizmann describes his success in this undertaking in the following words: "In the Commons, with such champions as Mr. Churchill and Major Ormsby-Gore, we had better luck, and a similar motion was heavily defeated." [58]

Though he had avoided disaster at the eleventh hour, however, Weizmann was forced to accept an inevitable setback. The British Government had to make some move to placate the objections to its pro-Zionist favoritism. On July 1, 1922, therefore, a statement of modified British policy on Zionism and Palestine was issued. This was known as the Churchill White Paper.[59] It denied that it was the intention of the British Government to create a wholly Jewish Palestine, and the Zionist representation in Palestine was neither to be assigned a special position nor to share in the general administration of the country. It also established the principle of economic absorptive capacity as far as Jewish immigration into Palestine was concerned, and eliminated Transjordan from Palestine.

Weizmann regarded the Churchill White Paper as a whittling down of the Balfour Declaration, but was willing to accept it inasmuch as it reaffirmed the right of the Jews to form a National Home in Palestine.[60] He also regarded the establishment of the principle of economic absorptive capacity as no real barrier to large scale Jewish immigration into Palestine, providing the Zionists saw to it that such economic absorptive capacity increased with the passage of time. Furthermore, the White Paper succeeded in defeating opposition to the Mandate in the British Parliament,[61] and on July 24, 1922, the Mandate was approved by that body.[62]

Weizmann was, above all, a political realist. During the Annual Conference of the World Zionist Organization held at Carlsbad in July and August of 1922, he met opposition to his acceptance of the Churchill White Paper. Many of the Zionists maintained that Weizmann should have held out for a Jewish charter, to which Weizmann replied that the White Paper existed, while the charter did not.[63] He always favored working with what was established instead of seeking to press impossible demands. This does not mean that he was willing to compromise Zionism, but that he saw the advantage in seeking fulfillment by stages. He saw also the wisdom of looking at political developments with complete realism. For example, his willingness not to press Zionist claims to Transjordan was coupled with the belief that Transjordan would later become an integral part of the Jewish State once the job of building Palestine had been completed. In a speech in Jerusalem in 1926, he asserted: "The road to Allenby Bridge along which we shall cross over to Trans-Jordan will not be paved by soldiers but by Jewish labor and the Jewish plough." [64] The basic aims of Zionism were never abandoned by him, but he was willing to compromise temporarily for the sake of ultimate success. He also considered short-run compromises as far from binding. Remarking once on the relative significance of declarations, statements, and instruments, he asserted that they were merely frames which might or might not be filled in. "They have virtually no importance unless and until they are supported by actual performance. . . ." [65]

The Churchill White Paper paved the way for the acceptance of the Mandate by the League, established the right of the Zionists to colonize Palestine, and generally opened the way for a substantial Zionist beginning in Palestine. British support was maintained, and the way was paved for Jewish immigration, another major requirement of Herzl's program. Zionism was next faced with the question of its own reorganization so that it could undertake the task ahead, and then with the problem of winning the support of world Jewry.

CHAPTER IV

THE GROWTH OF POLITICAL ZIONISM

Reorganization of the Movement

At the close of the First World War, the leaders of the Zionist Organization realized that an organizational machinery capable of handling the expanded operations of the movement was vitally needed. In February, 1919, Weizmann and Sokolow called a Zionist Conference in London.[1] At this meeting, Weizmann was appointed to the Executive, an honor which had not been extended to him before, even though he had served as *de facto* leader of the Zionist Organization for years. Also, a Central Office to be located in London was established. It took the place of the Zionist Bureau, which had been created in London after the issue of the Balfour Declaration for the purpose of undertaking the political work needed to assure that the Declaration was put into force. In effect, this Conference gave legal sanction to the *de facto* political office through which Weizmann and the other Zionist leaders in England had been operating. It set up a delegation to represent Zionism at the Peace Conference and to form one body out of the various Jewish delegations from different nations at the Peace Conference.[2]

In the summer of 1920, a second post-war Zionist Conference was convened at London. At this Conference, Weizmann was elected President of the Zionist Organization, thus confirming the *de facto* leadership he had exercised since the war years, and Nahum Sokolow, his lieutenant, was made chairman of the Executive.[3] The Conference also passed the following resolutions:[4] (1) the Organization is determined to live at peace with the non-Jewish communities in Palestine, (2) all land in Palestine colonized by Jews is eventually to become the common property of the Jewish people, (3) a Jewish National Fund will be established to employ voluntary contributions for the purpose of making the land of Palestine the common property of the Jewish people, and (4) a Central Immigration Office will be created in Palestine and Palestine Offices will be opened in all countries expected to furnish contingents of young immigrants.

Thus the Conference centered attention on the second requirement of the Herzlian program—the Jewish colonization of Palestine. The framework of what was to become an intricate immigration organization was provided, and a special fund was established to implement a land policy designed to go hand-in-hand with the immigration policy. A second fund, which had been created in 1917, was renamed Keren Hayesod, or Foundation Fund, and it was specified that 20% of the contributions to this fund were to be turned over to the Jewish National Fund.[5] Two-thirds of the remainder was to be invested in permanent national institutions or development enterprises in Palestine. Palestine was thus to be occupied gradually through Jewish immigration regulated by the Zionists and through land purchase under a system of national funds, likewise controlled by the Zionist Organization. The Conference's resolution to live at peace with the non-Jewish communities in Palestine must be viewed in the light of this program of planned acquisition.

The Conference of 1920 appointed a commission to call a Zionist Congress, and accordingly the first Zionist Congress since before the war—the 12th—was convened at Carlsbad in September, 1921.[6] The Congress confirmed most of the decisions of the Conference of 1920, and declared that the hostility of the Arabs would not weaken the resolve of Zionists to work for the fulfillment of the movement's aim. The Executive, or Inner Actions Committee, was divided into two sections, one of which was to sit in Palestine. The Actions Committee, or General Council, was to be made up of the members of the Executive and representatives of Keren Hayesod, the Jewish National Fund, and the Jewish Colonial Trust, a bank which had been founded in the early days of political Zionism to serve as the financial instrument of the Organization.[7] The institution of the Annual Conference was replaced by the creation of a Central Council, made up of the Actions Committee, representatives of the Separate Unions and the financial institutions, and officials connected with the functions of the Congress.

The 12th Zionist Congress came to a close with the confirmation of Weizmann as the President of the Organization and Sokolow as the President of the Executive.[8] At this point, Weizmann stood at the head of an elaborate organization which provided all the necessary offices for bringing the aim of political Zionism to fulfillment. Beneath him was a Central Office, the task of which was to maintain political contact with the Colonial Office of the British Government, thus providing the machinery with which to maintain British support and to oversee the activities of Zionists throughout the world. Under the Central Office was an executive group composed of the London and Palestine Executives, the Actions Committee, and the Central Council. The London offices maintained close relations with the League of Nations,[9] the French Government, and the Italian Government through Special Bureaus. They also controlled the colonization funds and were advised on financial matters by a Financial and Economic Council. The Palestine Executive replaced the Zionist Commission in Palestine and was charged with supervision of the Jewish community in Palestine[10] and Jewish immigration into the country.

To ensure that the Palestine Executive also maintained good relations with the British Administration, Weizmann arranged for the appointment of a British officer of Jewish faith to the Palestine Executive. At the end of 1922, Dr. Eder, leading light of the Palestine Executive, retired from office. In search of a replacement, Weizmann approached General Macdonough of British Military Intelligence, asking him to suggest a candidate—one ". . . belonging to both worlds, English as well as Jewish. . . ." [11] Macdonough suggested Colonel Fred Kisch, a member of Military Intelligence, a British officer in every sense, and the son of an East European Jew who had belonged to Choveve Zion. From every point of view, Kisch was the perfect man. He was acquainted with High Commissioner Samuel, he could hold the respect of the British officers in the Palestine Administration, he could feel at home with Zionists, and he was trained in Intelligence, the key to Zionist diplomacy. It is indeed strange that the question of dual loyalty never was brought up in the case of Kisch. Somehow Weizmann was always a genius at making what would ordinarily be considered unnatural seem innocuous and sensible.

With the establishment of a perfectly organized machine for the maintenance of the advantage gained with the British Government during the war years and the promotion of Jewish colonization of Palestine, Weizmann had succeeded in maintaining and reinforcing British support, and in laying the groundwork for the Jewish colonization of Palestine. He was next faced with the problem of fulfilling the third requirement of the Herzlian program—winning the support of world Jewry to the cause of political Zionism. Zionist Federations, Separate Unions, and Separate Societies were

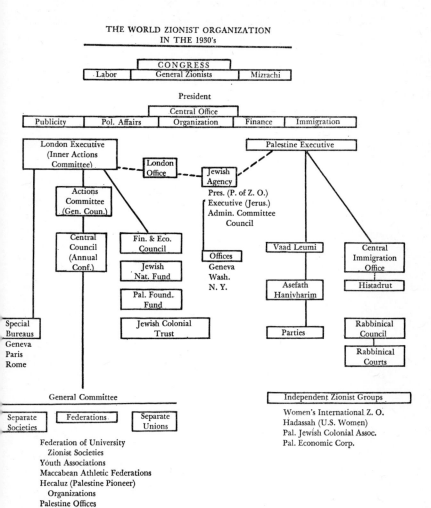

THE WORLD ZIONIST ORGANIZATION
IN THE 1930's

CONGRESS

| Labor | General Zionists | Mizrachi |

President

Central Office

| Publicity | Pol. Affairs | Organization | Finance | Immigration |

London Executive (Inner Actions Committee)

London Office

Jewish Agency
Pres. (P. of Z. O.)
Executive (Jerus.)
Admin. Committee
Council

Palestine Executive

Actions Committee (Gen. Coun.)

Central Council (Annual Conf.)

Fin. & Eco. Council

Jewish Nat. Fund

Pal. Found. Fund

Jewish Colonial Trust

Offices
Geneva
Wash.
N. Y.

Vaad Leumi

Asefath Hanivharim

Parties

Central Immigration Office

Histadrut

Rabbinical Council

Rabbinical Courts

Special Bureaus
Geneva
Paris
Rome

General Committee

| Separate Societies | Federations | Separate Unions |

Federation of University
  Zionist Societies
Youth Associations
Maccabean Athletic Federations
Hecaluz (Palestine Pioneer)
  Organizations
Palestine Offices

Independent Zionist Groups

Women's International Z. O.
Hadassah (U.S. Women)
Pal. Jewish Colonial Assoc.
Pal. Economic Corp.

already in existence in countries all over the world. But a mechanism was needed to recruit large groups of non-Zionist Jews. The Jewish Agency was chosen to fulfill this task.

Extending the Jewish Agency

The text of the Mandate for Palestine specified that ". . . an appropriate Jewish agency shall be recognised as a public body for the purpose of advising and co-operating with the Administration of Palestine in such economic, social and other matters as may affect the establishment of the Jewish national home and the interests of the Jewish population in Palestine. . . ."[12] The Zionist Organization was to serve as such an agency, according to the text of the Mandate. At the Zionist Conference held at Carlsbad in August and September of 1922, therefore, the Zionist Organization formally accepted the rights and duties of the Jewish Agency, expressing the wish that "the Jewish Agency shall represent the whole Jewish people." [13]

As an organ designed to assist in the fulfillment of the aim of political Zionism, the Jewish Agency could hardly be considered representative of a world Jewry which was far from being solidly Zionist. To Weizmann, however, the idea of extending the Jewish Agency presented itself as a perfect solution to the problem of fulfilling the third policy requirement of the Herzlian program—winning the support of world Jewry. He viewed the Palestine Foundation Fund as providing a link with Zionism for those willing to help but not to participate. But he saw that this was insufficient as a means of really recruiting the forces of international Jewry,[14] and therefore became a champion of the extension of the Jewish Agency.[15]

An obstacle stood before Weizmann and the realization of

his plan—the opposition to the extension of the Jewish Agency among Zionists. The Brandeis Group regarded the extension as unnecessary, and others feared the influence of non-Zionists in the Agency. Fortunately for Weizmann, however, the leadership of American Zionism had passed from the hands of Brandeis.[16] In February, 1923, the Actions Committee passed a resolution stating "that the controlling organ of the Jewish Agency shall be responsible to a body representative of the Jewish people."[17] At the same time, the Committee decided to enter into negotiations with leading Jewish communities in order to gain their participation in the Jewish Agency.[18] At the Congress of 1925, a party known as the Revisionists and led by Vladimir Jabotinsky opposed extension on the basis that Zionist policy could not be entrusted to Jews lacking strong nationalist convictions.[19] The Congress concluded, however, by passing a resolution favoring the establishment of a Council for the Jewish Agency composed equally of Zionist and non-Zionist Jews.[20] It was also specified that the Jewish Agency must base its activities on the following principles: (1) the development of a continuously increasing volume of Jewish immigration into Palestine, (2) the redemption of the land in Palestine as Jewish public property, (3) agricultural colonization based on Jewish labor, and (4) the promotion of Hebrew language and culture in Palestine.[21]

The way was now completely clear for the fulfillment of Weizmann's plan. The Congress had agreed to the extension of the Agency, even though the matter remained controversial until 1929, and specifications ensuring the fulfillment of Zionist policy were established. The Congress gave further guarantees by insisting that the President of the Zionist Organization become President of the enlarged Jewish Agency. It also stated that of the non-Zionist participants, 40% should be from America, which contained a large number of non-

45

Zionist Jews and therefore was a major objective in the Zionist bid for universal Jewish support.

In first laying his plans for the extension of the Jewish Agency, Weizmann reflected:[22]

> There were, it might seem, two ways of drawing into the work of Palestine those Jews who were not prepared to call themselves Zionists—two ways of creating the Agency. One was to organize a full-fledged 'World Jewish Congress' . . . . [the other was to] invite the various great organizations already at work in other fields to join us without forfeiting their identity. This second way was the one I proposed and ultimately carried into effect.

Once he had thus decided to recruit non-Zionist Jewish organizations to join in the work of the Agency and subsequently draw their followers unwittingly into the Zionist movement, Weizmann lost no time in concentrating his attention on the United States. He travelled there in 1923 and immediately approached the recognized leader of American Jewry—Louis Marshall.[23] He had maintained indirect contact with Marshall since 1919, and no introduction was necessary. Using the technique of convincing Marshall that he (Marshall) was the man of the hour for world Jewry, Weizmann effected his recruitment with comparative ease. He next approached Felix Warburg, another leader of American Jewry. Weizmann challenged the American to go to Palestine and see for himself the work that was being done by the colonists of Zionism.[24] Warburg took him up, was shown around Palestine by Fred Kisch, and returned a convinced Zionist. Of this Weizmann remarked, "I have seldom witnessed a more complete conversion."[25]

Through Marshall and Warburg, American Jewry began to join the Zionist movement, to assist in its work, and to bear much of its financial burden. It was for this reason that the Congress of 1925 specified that 40% of the non-Zionist representation on the Jewish Agency was to be American.

In 1927, Weizmann and Marshall formally agreed to the extension of the Jewish Agency in accordance with the terms of the Palestine Mandate and the resolutions of the Zionist Congresses.[26] Then, in 1929, the 16th Zionist Congress resolved in favor of the enlargement of the Agency and the establishment of an Agency Council and subordinate offices composed equally of Zionists and non-Zionists.[27] After the Congress, a Constituent Assembly of the new Agency convened, and the non-Zionists pledged to stand side by side with the Zionists in the work of Palestine. Marshall and Warburg assured Weizmann of financial and moral support from American Jewry.[28]

As a further assurance that the new Agency would not fall under non-Zionist control, the Zionists obtained a guarantee from the British Government to the effect that should the partnership between Zionists and non-Zionists dissolve, the Zionist Organization alone would be recognized as the Jewish Agency.[29] This assurance was hardly necessary, however, since by associating important non-Zionist Jewish groups with the development of the National Home in Palestine, the Zionists had succeeded in making them Zionist by implication. There was no return once the journey on such a path had been started. Furthermore, in carrying these influential groups along with them, a trend which was to bring enormous segments of world Jewry into the Zionist movement had been inaugurated. And it was not only in the United States that the spadework had been undertaken. In Weizmann's words, ". . . in every country with a Jewish population, the same story had played itself out."[30] The third requirement of Herzl's program was being gradually fulfilled, and the battle for Palestine was set in full motion.

CHAPTER V

ZIONIST STRATEGY IN THE 1930's

The decade of the 1920's was a period of preparation for the Zionists, not only in the matter of building up the machinery with which to implement their policies, but also in initiating the struggle for Palestine which came to a head in the 1930's.

In London, few problems arose after the ratification of the Mandate. The Conservatives were in power from October, 1922, to June, 1929, except for the brief period of the first MacDonald Ministry from January to November of 1924. The Conservatives stood by the Balfour Declaration,[1] and thus no obstacle was presented by the change of governments. In Geneva, the Permanent Mandates Commission began to become concerned over the problem of the Palestinian Arabs in 1924, but the Zionists opened a Special Bureau there in the following year, and "Gradually, succeeding sessions of the Mandates Commission were to show traces of its effect."[2] Also Weizmann's personal contacts with leading members of the Commission served to develop a favorable attitude toward Zionism in that body.[3]

In Palestine, Jewish immigration reached a high of 34,386 in 1925,[4] but slumped in the second half of the decade owing to conditions of local depression. Nevertheless, between September 1, 1920, and the end of 1929, 99,806 Jews immigrated to Palestine, while only 23,977 departed from the country.[5] After the issue of the Churchill White Paper in 1922, a Labor Schedule was established to regulate the immigration of Jewish workers in accordance with the economic absorptive capacity of Palestine.[6] The Zionist Organization guaranteed the support of many of the immigrants for the first year of their stay in Palestine,[7] and the Histadrut, or General Federation of Jewish Labor in Palestine, served as an employment agency for the newcomers.[8] In 1923, Jews possessing capital assets amounting to $2,500 or more were allowed to immigrate outside of the Labor Schedule.[9]

It is particularly interesting to note the attitude of Weizmann toward this Jewish immigration, since it shows the true character of political Zionism: ". . . we must see to it that we direct this stream," he said, "and do not allow it to deflect us from our goal."[10] The leaders and responsible officers of the Zionist movement have regarded themselves as a disciplined vanguard, an inner elite, of a movement which they consider the one answer to the Jewish Question. And their attitude, even towards Jews, has been colored by their zeal to complete the work of Zionism. Thus, they have been impatient with anything connected with Palestine which did not clearly contribute to the establishment of Jewish statehood, and resentful of those things which in any way acted against the interests of the movement.

Immediately following the conclusion of the 16th Zionist Congress and the Constituent Assembly of the enlarged Jewish Agency, Arab-Jewish rioting broke out in Jerusalem and other cities as a result of a religious dispute over the Wailing Wall in Jerusalem. The Shaw Commission, which investigated the riots, blamed the Arabs for starting the trouble, but echoed the opinion of the Haycraft Commission that the underlying cause was Arab opposition to the Jewish National Home and to Jewish immigration.[11] The Commission charged that Jewish immigration authorities had departed from the doctrine accepted by the Zionist Organization in 1922.[12]

Weizmann was disturbed by the recommendations for more stringent control of immigration made by the Shaw Commission and feared that Zionism would be blocked in the work of building up a Jewish majority in Palestine. After the report was issued, he arranged an introduction to Ramsay MacDonald, the new Labor Prime Minister, through the good offices of Lady Astor.[13] The introduction was effected in Geneva, and Weizmann not only received a pledge of support from MacDonald, but also from M. Aristide Briand of France.

Subsequently, however, the British Government dispatched Sir John Hope Simpson to Palestine to look into the whole matter of Jewish immigration. Simpson concluded that Jewish colonization had caused the displacement of many Arabs.[14] His Report was accompanied by a new declaration of British policy known as the Passfield White Paper. This White Paper asserted that in the matter of Palestine ". . . a double undertaking is involved, to the Jewish people on the one hand and the non-Jewish population of Palestine on the other."[15] It also stated that "Any hasty decision in regard to more unrestricted Jewish immigration is to be strongly deprecated. . . ."[16]

The Zionists were up in arms at this turn of events, and immediately moved into action to stem the tide. Weizmann resigned as President of the Jewish Agency, and "Then began an intense struggle with the Colonial Office. . . ."[17] All the sympathizers of Zionism, including Lloyd George, General Smuts, Baldwin, and Chamberlain, lifted their voices in protest, and the issue was debated in Commons.[18] The upshot of the ensuing Zionist propaganda campaign—which set a precedent for the development of a new Zionist technique because of its size and success—was the decision of

MacDonald to bring committees from the Jewish Agency and the British Cabinet together to discuss the situation.[19] In spite of his resignation, Weizmann was on the committee from the Jewish Agency, which was largely under his direction.

There were two points upon which Weizmann sought to obtain the agreement of the Cabinet committee.[20] The first of these was that the obligation of the mandatory was not to 170,000 Jews as opposed to 700,000 Arabs, but to the Jewish people. Thus he wanted the Cabinet to agree that its moral obligation to the Jews justified what would ordinarily be thought of as an immoral lack of consideration for the Arab majority in Palestine. The second point was that the promise of the Jewish National Home could not yet be considered as fulfilled. This was another way of saying that restrictions should not be placed on Jewish immigration. At the same time, Weizmann tried to convince the Cabinet committee that it had always been the Arabs who were responsible for trouble in Palestine.[21]

As a result of the effectiveness of the Zionist propaganda campaign, and through political pressure applied on Mac-Donald by Jewish labor leaders,[22] the Prime Minister virtually repudiated the Passfield White Paper. This he did through an official letter to Weizmann dated February 13, 1931.[23] Weizmann summarizes the significance of the letter in the following words:

> . . . it was under MacDonald's letter to me that the change came about in the Government's attitude, and in the attitude of the Palestine administration, which enabled us to make the magnificent gains of the ensuing years. It was under MacDonald's letter that Jewish immigration into Palestine was permitted to reach figures like forty thousand for 1934 and sixty-two thousand for 1935, figures undreamed of in 1930.[24]

51

As if the reversal of policy by MacDonald was not enough, Weizmann's success was topped by the appointment of Sir Arthur Wauchope as High Commissioner to Palestine. The appointment was made by MacDonald in consultation with Weizmann, and it was under Wauchope that Zionism made its great strides in Palestine.[25]

As in the past, a setback to Zionism incurred by the report of a commission which was sent to see for itself the cause of the troubles of Palestine was reversed by the activity of Zionist diplomacy in London. Through propaganda, political pressure, and the use of the recruits of Zionism in high places, a government policy decision based on the findings of its own commission was reversed. To those who might wonder why it is that the commissions always seem to be firm with Zionism while the Cabinets are so easily moved to do Zionism's bidding in times of crisis, the answer has already been given. Those who went to see the real situation realized that as Zionism was attaining its goal, there was an accompanying breach in the provision of the Balfour Declaration regarding the rights of the non-Jewish community of Palestine. Thus, they voiced their objections, remaining true to the Declaration they were pledged to uphold. The Cabinets, on the other hand, either did not grasp what was going on or were forced to look the other way because of the pressure that was being applied. The Zionist Organization of the 1930's was not like the Zionist Organization of the war years. In those earlier days it had to wait for its friends to come to power, but in the 1930's it did not hesitate to bend even a Prime Minister to its will, if that was necessary.

The Zionist success in 1931 led almost immediately to greatly increased Jewish immigration into Palestine. In 1933, the Jewish immigration figures rose to 30,327 and in 1935

52

twice that number were admitted.[26] In November of 1935 the five Arab parties of Palestine presented the following demands to the Administration: (1) the creation of a democratic parliament, (2) the prohibition of land sales, and (3) the cessation of immigration.[27] The High Commissioner responded by announcing that he had been authorized to establish a Legislative Council.[28] The previous summer the Zionist Congress had declared its opposition to the creation of a Legislative Council, since such an institution would reduce the Jews of Palestine to the status of a minority,[29] and consequently, the Palestinian Jews refused to offer their cooperation.[30] In April of 1936, the Arab Palestinians precipitated a general strike, and the British Government appointed a Royal Commisssion to investigate the trouble.[31]

The Report of the Royal Commission, which was published in July, 1937, attributed the cause of the disturbances to the desire of the Arabs for national independence and the hatred and fear of the establishment of the Jewish National Home.[32] It proposed the partition of Palestine as the only solution to the Arab-Jewish problem. The Pan-Arab Congress held at Bludan, Syria, in September, 1937, rejected the partition plan,[33] while the Zionist Congress which met in August, 1937, authorized the Executive to enter into negotiations with the British Government as to the creation of a Jewish state in Palestine.[34] Weizmann favored partition as a step in the right direction,[35] but disagreement among the members of a commission sent to define the partition boundaries in 1938,[36] and the continuation of Arab rebellion[37] doomed the scheme to failure.

With war clouds looming over the European horizon, the British called the London Conference in 1939 to try to settle the Arab-Jewish controversy. The famous MacDonald White Paper, issued on May 17, 1939, imposed severe restrictions on Jewish immigration.[38] The Zionist Congress held the following fall declared the White Paper illegal, but very soon afterwards the world was caught up by a second global war, and the question of Palestine was placed in abeyance. Thus ended the second phase in the story of the diplomacy of Zionism.

CHAPTER VI

THE REORIENTATION OF POLITICAL ZIONISM

Policy

The issue of the MacDonald White Paper in 1939 brought to a close another chapter in the history of political Zionism. That chapter had opened following the Zionist victory in the struggle over the Mandate, and ran its course throughout the remainder of the inter-war period. It was a phase characterized by a gradual forwarding of Zionism's aims as a result of the continuing successes of Zionist diplomacy with the British and the development of a Zionist organizational machinery capable of fulfilling the requirements of Herzl's program. The 1939 White Paper, however, came as a major setback to Zionist diplomacy, and the leaders of the movement immediately sought a reorientation of Zionism in the face of the new turn of events. Throughout the war years, just such a reorientation took place in terms of policy, organization, and of a shift in political concentration from Great Britain to the United States.

During the inter-war period, the Mandate for Palestine had served the interests of the Zionists by permitting a gradual build-up of the Jewish community in Palestine, a process which would have resulted in the eventual establishment of a Jewish majority in the country, had it not been for the MacDonald White Paper. Consequently, the White Paper threw into question the policy of gradualism championed by

Weizmann. The Mandate now had not only ceased to be of service to Zionism, but even threatened to thwart the fulfillment of one of Zionism's primary aims—the creation of a Jewish majority in Palestine through immigration. This called for a change of policy—not an alteration of those aims and basic policies which have remained consistent since Herzl, but a new attitude toward the Mandate. Previously the Mandate had been supported because its existence was consonant with the desires of Zionism, but once the British showed an unwillingness to continue their benign attitude toward the Zionists, the latter turned against their former benefactors and decided to work actively for the termination of the Mandate for Palestine.[1]

Throughout the war years, the Zionist leaders developed a coordinated program of opposition to the Mandate's continuation. The widespread agitation of Zionists throughout the world and of the Jewish community in Palestine seems to reflect this planned campaign of the leadership.[2] In October of 1939, David Ben Gurion, a leading Palestinian Zionist, announced that Zionism's new policy must be based on an insistence that Jewish immigration be increased and Jewish land holdings extended.[3] Weizmann echoed the same sentiment in New York the following January, when he outlined Zionism's immediate mission as one of employing every opportunity to effect a revocation of the MacDonald White Paper.[4]

These initial attacks on the White Paper soon enlarged to assume the form of an onslaught against the Mandate itself. The first indication of this important policy shift was given by Dr. Weizmann, who, ironically enough, had in the past been the strongest backer of cooperation with the Mandate. In mid-December, 1939, Weizmann called on Winston Churchill at the Admiralty and announced that after the war the Zionists would want to build up a state of three to four million Jews in Palestine.[5] Churchill, whose established sympathy with Zionism is reminiscent of that of Lord Balfour and Lloyd George, replied that such a plan met entirely with his approval. With this preliminary agreement, Zionism began to depart from a phase of advantageous waiting and to enter one characterized by active preparation for the fulfillment of the basic aim of Zionism—the creation of the Jewish State.

It is often assumed that this change in Zionist policy represented the emergence of a position intermediate between the traditional policy of Weizmann and the outlook of the Revisionists, a development which supposedly resulted spontaneously out of the disappointment of Zionists with ". . . the policy of conciliation which had guided the Zionist leadership in its dealings with Great Britain."[6] It is difficult to support this view in the light of the fact that the Mandate had done far more to serve the interests of Zionism than to impede those interests. Furthermore, Weizmann himself was one of the first to suggest the new policy, a stand which he reasserted more openly in early 1942.[7] It therefore seems more realistic to assume that the shift in Zionist policy from cooperation with to hostility against the British was dictated primarily by a change in circumstances which made a policy of activism more useful than any other for the realization of Zionism's aims. It has already been noted that these aims and basic policies have remained consistent and united in purpose since the early days of the movement, but that the Zionist leaders have always shown great flexibility in their formulation of operational policies. The prime consideration in these matters has been practicality, for whatever served the ultimate goals was acceptable to the movement.

Zionism's new policy of activism reached maturity in the early 1940's. At the beginning of 1940, Ben Gurion informed the General Officer Commanding in Palestine that he had no intention of taking any active steps to help end the disturbances then taking place among the Jewish community.[8] This same attitude was promoted by Ben Gurion in March of 1943, when he stated before Jewish leaders in Palestine: ". . . there will be no cooperation between us and the White Paper authorities. . . . We are preparing our own plans. . . ."[9]

This preparation of active opposition to the Mandate in Palestine was paralleled by a campaign in the West—and particularly in America—designed to reorient Zionist members in the Diaspora to the new policy. In early 1940, a conference in Washington was informed by the President of the Jewish National Fund that the policy of the Fund was to preclude any possible partition of Palestine by purchasing frontier areas,[10] implying thereby that the time had come to pave the way for the establishment of the Jewish State in all of Palestine. A year later, a similar proclamation was made before a convention of Canadian Zionists by the legal adviser of the Jewish Agency, Dr. Bernard Joseph.[11] Also at this time, a conference of the United Palestine Appeal meeting in Washington resolved that with the termination of the war, a Jewish state should be established in Palestine.[12] Shortly after—on March 29, 1941—Dr. Weizmann announced at Chicago that after the war a Jewish commonwealth could be set up side by side with an Arab Federation in the Middle East.[13]

These and similar proclamations served to imbue Western Zionist Jewry with an activist spirit and to gear its thinking to the idea of the imminent establishment of Israel as a state once the war was finished. The leadership was successful in this endeavor, and in the United States, for example, the Zionist Organization of America resolved as early as September 7, 1941, to demand the creation of a Jewish commonwealth within the historic boundaries of Palestine.[14]

But more than this was required. It was necessary for a

significant body of the Zionist Diaspora to convene at a suitable place and proclaim unanimously the decision of world Zionism to bid for the establishment of Israel upon the completion of the war. The Emergency Committee was readily willing to sponsor the convention,[15] and therefore called an extraordinary conference of American, European, and Palestinian Zionists, which was held at the Biltmore Hotel in New York City in May of 1942.

The Extraordinary Zionist Conference was addressed by three of the top leaders of Zionism:[16] Weizmann, Ben Gurion, and Nahum Goldmann, chairman of the administrative committee of the World Jewish Congress. Of particular importance were the pronouncements of Ben Gurion, whose position at this time was that of political leader of the Palestine Executive of the Jewish Agency.[17] Ben Gurion's main demands were that the Jewish Agency be awarded full control over immigration into Palestine and that the concept of binationalism be discarded if it entailed offering Palestinian Arabs equal representation with Jews in the departments of government.[18] Here, then, was a fundamental presentation of the new Zionist policy, for the realization of such a program could lead to only one outcome—the creation of a Jewish state. The Conference took the lead that Ben Gurion offered it, and the participants expressed their desire to insist on "a full implementation of the Basle program."[19] Thus, the underlying clarity of purpose that has always remained with political Zionism now came to the surface, and there remained only the task of formulating the already planned new policy of activism and open preparation for the fulfillment of the primary aim of the Herzlian program.

On May 11, the Conference adopted a set of resolutions known collectively as the Biltmore Program,[20] and containing within them the basic platform of Zionism's new policy. In summary, the portions dealing with this policy called for the following: (1) recognition that the purpose of the pro-visions in the Balfour Declaration and the Mandate declaring the historic connection of the Jewish people with Palestine was to found there a Jewish commonwealth,[21] (2) the invalidation of the MacDonald White Paper, (3) a solution of the problem of Jewish homelessness as part of the post-war settlement (here implying that the Zionist solution was the only solution), (4) the transfer of control of immigration into Palestine to the Jewish Agency (thus giving that Agency one of the essential powers of a sovereign government), and (5) the establishment of Palestine as a Jewish commonwealth.

The Biltmore Program not only gave an indispensable quality of prestige to the new policy of the Zionist leadership, but also served to bring the great majority of world Zionism positively behind the platform of imminent statehood. In October, 1942, the Zionist Organization of America and Hadassah officially adopted the Biltmore Program, and the Mizrachi and Labor groups subsequently did likewise, though later the Labor organization did not specifically rule out the possibility of bi-nationalism.[22] Then, on November 6, the General Council[23] of the World Zionist Organization endorsed the Program,[24] thus rendering the new activism an official plank of Zionism at large, even though no Congress had been convened to debate such an important decision.[25] When the first post-war Zionist conference was held in August, 1945, the thinking of such a large majority of the Zionists had been geared to the Biltmore Program that it was strongly endorsed.[26]

Centering Activity in America

Aside from the formulation of a new policy, the war years witnessed a significant change in the Zionists' basic plan of attack. Since the beginning of World War I, political Zionism had realized Gentile support, a basic concern of the Herzlian program, by obtaining the assistance of the British Government through the recruitment of cabinet ministers and other British political leaders. Following the publication of the 1939 White Paper and the formulation of a new Zionist policy, however, the Zionist attitude toward Great Britain underwent a fundamental change. Now the British Government—and the Colonial Office and the Mandate authorities in particular—was regarded as an enemy, a hindrance to the fulfillment of the basic aim of Zionism.

It was for this reason that the Zionist leaders turned to the United States. At first, they sought to bring American pressure to bear on British policy[27] in an attempt to effect a reversal of the White Paper and attain British acceptance of a program of Jewish statehood to be established after the war. Later in the war, however, many Zionists began to feel that Britain was losing her position as a first class power, and they therefore turned to the United States as the primary source of Gentile support for Zionism.[28] In the past, America had proved to be a valuable source of financial assistance to the movement, but during the war it also emerged as the new center from which political help was to be sought. As a result, America became the focal point of Zionist political activity during the war, even though Britain continued to hold a place of importance, since the Mandate for Palestine was still hers. It is interesting to note at this point that the very Zionist Organization upon which many British statesmen had once pinned their hopes for strategic and political support of British interests in the Middle East was now turning with little hesitation away from that Power without whose help the Zionist movement would long since have been relegated to the realm of theory. Zionism shifted its interest from Britain to America with that facile flexibility that has always characterized the movement.

Related to Zionism's policy reorientation and political concentration in America was the wartime organization of the movement. As has already been mentioned, the Jewish Agency was converted into a Zionist body, owing to the breakdown in its administrative machinery in 1939. This development, however, was only meaningful in the sense that it served to give an added cohesion and integration to Zionism at a time when the prevailing international uncertainty called for close organization and full freedom of action. Furthermore, the policy change previously described had been formulated by the leadership already in the fall of 1939, and since the new policy was more extreme than the old, no chances could be taken with the more moderate non-Zionist groups which had participated in the Jewish Agency. Indeed, this precaution proved to be well taken from the Zionist point of view, for when the new policy was proclaimed in the Biltmore Program, many of the moderate Jewish groups in the West voiced their protest.[29] Even though the conversion of the Jewish Agency was not meaningful in the sense that the Zionist Organization had always maintained an effective control over the Agency, it would still have been embarrassing to have dissension in a body which the Zionists were employing to present Zionism as having the support of world Jewry.

At the same time that this reintegration of the Jewish Agency into the Zionist Organization was taking place, another move was made to keep the movement closely knit during the war years. At a meeting of the Executive in Geneva in August of 1939, the members of the American delegation combined with the leaders of the World Zionist Organization to set up an organization which could serve as alternate headquarters for the movement and maintain contact with those groups which might find themselves cut off from the London and Palestine Executives.[30] This organization was named the Emergency Committee, and was later reorganized and entitled the American Zionist Emergency Council.

The Emergency Council served two important functions. First, it provided a good wartime headquarters through which the leadership could project its new policy. The Council was composed of the major American General Zionist groups (Zionist Organization of America and Hadassah) as well as Zionist Labor and Mizrachi factions.[31] It was therefore representative of the primary Zionist component parties. At the same time, the World Zionist leadership could maintain an important element of control over the Emergency Council through the appointment by Dr. Weizmann of a number of Zionist leaders to the Council on behalf of the Jewish Agency Executive.[32] The Emergency Council served as Zionist headquarters during the war and played a particularly important role in precipitating the new policy, for it was the Council which called the extraordinary conference at the Biltmore in the spring of 1942.[33]

The second important function of the Emergency Council was to facilitate the concentration of the Zionist leadership on the United States and to pave the way for the transfer of Zionism's center in the Gentile world from Britain to America. It coordinated the Zionist work in the United States[34] and prepared the organizational machinery which was to play such an important role in the history of Zionism during and after the war. America had already emerged as the leading country in the West, and if America could be won to the Zionist cause as England had been in the past, Zionism could soon achieve its ultimate goal of statehood.

Once the Emergency Council was established, there remained only the minor task of shifting the responsibility

63

for the intended policy change from the Jewish Agency to the Council, so that American Zionists might appear to be the center of the movement and the sponsors of the new policy. This was neatly maneuvered by the appointment of a Committee at the end of 1941 for the purpose of outlining the aims of the Jewish Agency.[35] This Committee then decided to obtain American approval of its deliberations before submitting them to the Inner General Council in Jerusalem, the supreme Zionist policy-making body during the war.[36] Once this move had been made, the American Zionist Emergency Council called the extraordinary conference, which in turn led to the Biltmore Program and the inauguration of the new policy of active preparation for statehood.

The organizational and policy-reorientation of Zionism that took place during the early part of the war provided the framework through which the Zionist leadership embarked on a new era in the movement's history. But also during this period, Zionist political operations continued as in the past. It is to these operations and the successes they effected for Zionism that we now turn.

CHAPTER VII

WARTIME ZIONIST DIPLOMACY IN BRITAIN AND PALESTINE

Operations in Great Britain

Although the Zionists turned increasingly to America for Gentile support during the war years, Great Britain continued to remain an important center of Zionist operations, for the Mandate was still Britain's charge. Throughout the war, Dr. Weizmann and other leaders of the movement worked tirelessly to further Zionism's fundamental policies. Having lost the sympathy of the Government temporarily following the issue of the 1939 White Paper, they sought once again to develop and maintain an effective pro-Zionist orientation at the focal points of political power. Simultaneously, they devised ways to manipulate public opinion in support of Zionism, and thereby to facilitate the more crucial operations in high places. They also continued the perennial Zionist attempt to gain the support of those Jews outside the movement, and waged a successful campaign against the forces of anti-Zionist British Jewry. Finally, they continued to seek means of maintaining a sizeable Jewish immigration into Palestine in spite of the White Paper restrictions.

The 1939 White Paper was issued by the Chamberlain Government, and so long as that Government was in power, it was subjected to severe Zionist criticism,[1] even though

Weizmann maintained contact with the higher administrative officials, including Foreign Secretary Lord Halifax.[2] The Zionists accomplished as little with this cabinet, however, as they had with that of Herbert Asquith during the First World War. They therefore adopted a waiting tactic, just as they had in 1915,[3] and sought to groom potential cabinet ministers for the future. For example, it was during this period that Weizmann called on Winston Churchill at the Admiralty and succeeded in obtaining the future Prime Minister's approval of Jewish statehood to be established after the war.[4]

With the establishment of the Coalition Government under Churchill in May of 1940, the Zionists were afforded the chance for which they had been waiting to seek a reversal of the White Paper policy and gradually work for an acceptance of the proposal for post-war Jewish statehood. Not only was Churchill himself a Zionist sympathizer, but also several other cabinet ministers were old friends of the Zionist cause.[5] For the remainder of the war, the Zionists employed this advantage at the summit of government to more than offset the opposition they met from the Colonial Office and the Mandate Administration. During the friction over illegal immigration in the fall of 1940,[6] for example, the Zionists not only succeeded in overcoming the opposition of British Mandate and Colonial Office authorities, who were simply carrying out their duties under the law, but also discredited those authorities by accusing them of embarrassing the Churchill Government and working against the true desires of the British people and their elected leaders, who were preoccupied with prosecuting the war.[7]

A sample case in which the Zionists had their way, in spite of the existing regulations and the non-partisan attitude of those charged with the enforcement of the regulations, was the Patria affair.[8] In November, 1940, nearly 2,000 illegal

66

Jewish immigrants were placed on a ship named the S.S. Patria at Haifa for deportation to a British island colony in the Indian Ocean. The Patria subsequently exploded with the loss of some 250 immigrants, but what is significant in this affair from the point of view of this study is the fact that the survivors were eventually allowed to enter the country, thus violating the then existing regulations, which were perhaps not so inhumane when viewed with the understanding that they were made to protect the non-Jewish community and not to persecute Jews. The story of how the Zionists got around the law in this case is carefully told by Weizmann in his autobiography:[9]

> One of the worst cases—that of the *Patria*—occurred during the war under the Colonial Secretaryship of Lord Lloyd; and on hearing of it I went to him . . . to try and persuade him to give permission for the passengers to be landed. . . .
>
> My arguments were wasted. Lord Lloyd could not agree with me. He said so, and added: 'I must tell you that I've blocked all the approaches for you. I know you will go to Churchill and try to get him to overrule me. I have therefore warned the Prime Minister that I will not consent. So please don't try to get at him.'
>
> But it seemed that Lord Lloyd had not blocked the approach to the Foreign Office, so I went to see Lord Halifax. . . . . To my intense relief and joy I heard the next day that he had sent a telegram to Palestine to permit the passengers to land.

Though this case is minor in the quantitative sense, it was important in discrediting the consistency of the British regulations and in contributing to the collapse of the White Paper policy.

This kind of Zionist operation on the highest levels of government was paralleled by attempts to make the best use of pro-Zionist Members of Parliament and to encourage the enunciation of party planks favoring the new Zionist policy of imminent statehood. The London Office of the Jewish Agency kept in touch with the pro-Zionists in Parliament by means of an organization known as the Parliamentary Palestine Committee, which was founded before the war.[10] At the same time, Weizmann and other Zionist leaders were constantly pressing their case with Labor Party leaders,[11] and on numerous occasions during the war, the Labor Party passed resolutions expressing sympathy with Zionism.[12]

Zionist political operations were supplemented by a broad propaganda campaign, the underlying design of which was to instigate a public demand for the abrogation of the MacDonald White Paper.[13] Taking advantage of the general ignorance of the Palestine question among Gentiles, the Zionists suggested the adoption of the Biltmore Program as the logical means of abrogating the White Paper, thus committing the receptive members of their audience to support Jewish statehood as a rider to their decision to oppose the White Paper. Actually, of course, the Biltmore Program and the White Paper remained two separate issues, but most Gentiles knew too little about the situation to make the distinction. The information section of the Jewish Agency's London Office was expanded in late 1941 to direct this campaign, and committees were established throughout the country to serve as propaganda outlets.[14]

The opposition of non-Zionist Jewry—particularly in Great Britain—had always remained a thorn in the side of political Zionism. It will be remembered, for example, that it was non-Zionist British Jews who insisted that the Balfour Declaration include provisions protecting the rights of the non-Jewish community of Palestine and of Jews outside Palestine. Twenty-five years later, however, the Zionists were stronger and felt that Jewish opposition at a time when the idea of a Jewish state was to be sold could not be tolerated. They therefore adopted two plans of action, one to swell the ranks of Zionism and the other to eliminate effective opposition by non-Zionist British Jewry. The British Zionist Federation launched a membership campaign which multiplied its numbers by five.[15] The non-Zionist Jews were dealt with with the same alacrity. Fortunately for the Zionists, the Board of Deputies of British Jews, the oldest group of its type in the country, developed a Zionist majority in 1943. Immediately, it became a Zionist instrument and little concern was shown for those who chose to retain the non-Zionist position. The Board's association with the Anglo-Jewish Association was severed, and in the fall of 1944, the Board endorsed the Biltmore Program.[16] Though the non-Zionists withdrew and formed an organization of their own, the back of Jewish opposition to Zionism in Britain had been broken, and an important step in the fulfillment of the third phase of the Herzlian program was taken.

In their search for approval of the Biltmore Program the Zionists employed in England a gambit which did much to serve the cause of Jewish nationality. In the early days of the war, Weizmann footnoted his pledges of Zionist support for the Allies, a matter in which no Jew really had any choice, with demands that independent Jewish units be formed to serve with the Allied armies.[17] On the surface, such a request seemed innocuous enough, but the underlying intentions were for the proposed fighting force to serve Zionism in two distinct ways. First, the recruitment of Palestinian Jews into military units would help form the nucleus of a Jewish army which could contend with Arab opposition when Jewish statehood was proclaimed. The second aim, which was more important in the political sense, was for the Jewish units to represent the Jewish people officially and fight under the banner of a Jewish

69

flag.[18] This would secure a significant recognition of the principle of Jewish statehood and serve as a step in the *de facto* recognition of Israel. It also would deal an effective blow to the non-Zionist Jews by creating the illusion that the Jews were participating in the war as members of the Jewish nation, not as citizens of Gentile nations, which was actually the case.

Because of the potential value to Zionism of the creation of a Jewish fighting force, Weizmann worked persistently throughout the war years to get the project approved. On December 1, 1939, Weizmann proposed that the Jewish Agency recruit a division of Jews.[19] The British Government was wary of the implications inherent in the creation of such a division and insisted that all Palestinian units be made up of Arabs as well as Jews. The following summer, Weizmann wrote to Churchill, urging him to reconsider the creation of Jewish units, especially since an occupation of Palestine by the Germans would place the Jews of the country at the mercy of Arab and Nazi hostility.[20] Churchill responded favorably, and in September, 1940, Weizmann, carrying with him the outline of a proposed program for the arming of Palestinian Jewry, attended a luncheon party given by the Prime Minister.[21]

The outline was worked over by those attending the luncheon, and the final formula, though it was not exactly what Weizmann wanted, contained certain specific concessions to the Zionists. Though the program maintained the principle of parity as to the number of Jews and Arabs to be recruited, a provision inserted at the insistence of the Colonial Office, it also called for "recruitment of the greatest possible number of Jews in Palestine for the fighting services, to be formed into Jewish battalions or larger formations." [22] Although only small numbers of Jews were recruited to form Jewish units, owing to the slowness of Arab enlistment, the creation of any entirely Jewish units was regarded by Zionists ". . . as a victory of a principle . . . . specific Jewish fighting units will take their places beside the British and their Allies. . . . They will fight as Jews and will represent the Jewish people—its living political nucleus in Palestine, as well as the great masses of Jews throughout the world."[23]

This important beginning in the Zionist struggle for the establishment of a Jewish fighting force was followed up by a campaign in 1942, '43, and '44 designed to overcome the limitations placed on Jewish recruitment by the parity clause and to expand the existing units of Palestinian Jews into a sizeable force consisting exclusively of Jews, who could join in the Allied struggle against Germany and represent Jewish nationality. In the summer of 1942, pro-Zionist members in both houses of Parliament proposed the creation of a Jewish Army, consisting of Palestinians and Jewish refugees from Europe.[24] Though these proposals did not materialize, they were probably instrumental in effecting the subsequent relaxation of the parity regulations.[25]

The continuing Zionist agitation for the establishment of a Jewish Army—in the United States as well as in Great Britain—met its ultimate success in September, 1944. On the twentieth of that month, the British War Office announced that it had decided to assist in the formation of a Jewish Brigade.[26] The Brigade, which later saw action in Italy, was awarded its own flag,[27] thus allowing it to parade Jewish nationality and to associate the fact of being Jewish with that nationality. Significantly, the flag of the Brigade is the flag of Israel today.

The Brigade also accomplished the other mission the Zionists had planned for it. In the words of a Zionist supporter, "The veterans of the Jewish Brigades became, exactly as the [Mandate] Administration had foreseen, the nucleus of the future Israeli Army and the decisive factor in the

71

Arab defeat, which, as things were, amounted to a defeat of British policy."[28] This was scarcely anticipated by those who during the First World War had envisioned Zionism as a prospective ally of British interests in the Middle East. One is compelled to question the validity of Zionist criticism of the Colonial Office and the Mandate Administration when one hears a Zionist frankly admit that creation of the Jewish Brigade, which was solicited with exclamations of the service it could perform for Britain and the Allies, ultimately served only to defeat British policy.

While the Zionists were pursuing their ends with such success in Great Britain, they also succeeded in drawing Prime Minister Churchill closer to support of the Biltmore Program. In the long run, this was of less significance, since the Labor Party came to power in 1945 and the new Foreign Minister was less cooperative with the Zionists. Nevertheless, it merits attention.

In October of 1944, the month after the announcement about the Jewish Brigade, the London Office of the Jewish Agency requested the British Government to designate Palestine as a Jewish commonwealth, and to permit the entry of one and one half million Jews into the country so that a sufficient majority could be established to proclaim the state.[29] A year earlier, Weizmann had received assurances from Churchill as to the latter's attitude toward Zionism.[30] Then, shortly after the 1944 memorandum to the British Government, Weizmann discussed the proposed plan more carefully with the Prime Minister.[31] At this meeting, Weizmann succeeded in obtaining Churchill's general consent to the idea of Jewish statehood, though perhaps not in all of Palestine. Had the Conservatives remained in power, however, it is likely that the British Government would have given recognition to Zionist claims of statehood in at least a restricted part of Palestine. As it was, the big post-war fight of Zionism took place in America, and it was Zionist operations in that country during the war that paved the way for this last battle before Israel's birth.

Activism in Palestine

The story of Jewish activism in Palestine does not properly fall within the scope of this study. However, there are certain facets of the activism—namely, the promotion of illegal immigration and the clandestine procurement of arms—which are related to the overall Zionist strategy of this period. The activity of the terrorists cannot be attributed to the Zionist leadership, and on numerous occasions, Weizmann and others decried the operations of the Irgun and the Sternists. Nevertheless, it should be noted that Ben Gurion refused to take any action against Jewish agitators in the early part of the war, and that after the conclusion of hostilities the Jewish Agency worked in collusion with the terrorists.[32]

Inasmuch as the Zionists chose to regard the 1939 White Paper as illegal, they felt no moral compunction about sponsoring the unauthorized immigration of Jews into Palestine. During the war, Zionist propaganda blamed much of the plight of European Jews on the absence of a Jewish state.[33] Many of the refugees were drawn to Zionism, owing to their desperate situation and the effectiveness of the Zionist propaganda, and a number of them sought refuge in Palestine. The Zionists were very willing to assist them. The Vaad Leumi had drawn up plans for a coordinated Jewish resistance to the White Paper,[34] a program which appears to have been devoted largely to the sponsorship of illegal immigration. Also, the Jewish Agency established a United Rescue Committee, which succeeded in settling 10,000 Jews in Palestine through cooperation with the Jewish underground in Europe.[35] The latter was known as the

Mossad le Aliyah Bet (Committee for Illegal Immigration) and was organized in 1937.[36]

This activist campaign designed to maintain a substantial flow of Jews into Palestine in spite of the White Paper limitations resulted in a number of unfortunate incidents in which shiploads of illegal immigrants were turned away or deported by the Mandate authorities.[37] On two occasions, refugee-bearing ships exploded and sank, with tragic loss of life; and in general, the fortune of the refugees who chose to attempt illegal entry into Palestine was far from pleasant. One Mandate official commented that the British Government was not lacking in sympathy for those who had fled from Nazi tyranny, but asserted at the same time that the immigrants had attempted to enter Palestine ". . . against what is well known to be the law of the country." [38]

But it was the Zionists who had promoted the illegal immigration, and it was they who knew the situation and must bear the primary responsibility for the fate of the refugees. On the surface, it is difficult to understand why the Zionists should subject members of their own race, whose plight had already been so tragic, to the frustrations of attempting illegal entry into Palestine. But it becomes understandable when it is realized that to the ardent Zionist the fulfillment of Herzl's program is the overriding concern. Commenting on American Jewish philanthropy for European Jewry during and after the First World War, Weizmann reflects in his autobiography: ". . . for one who believed that the Jewish homeland offered the only substantial and abiding answer to the Jewish problem, their [the American Jewish philanthropists] faith in the ultimate restabilizing of European Jewry was a tragedy. It was heart-breaking to see them pour millions into a bottomless pit, when some of the money could have been directed to the Jewish Homeland.

. . . ."[39] This is the explanation of why the Zionists in World War II did not always consider the comfort of the harassed Jews of Europe who had followed the advice of the Zionists and gone to Palestine in good faith, but illegally.

Zionist activism was also apparent in Palestine during the war in connection with illegal procurement of arms. Though the Jewish Agency outwardly cooperated with the Mandate authorities, it was simultaneously coordinating a program of illegal arms acquisition by means of theft from British supplies.[40] Subsequent British repression of these activities evoked accusations of anti-Semitism, a characteristic Zionist reaction to anything which works against the interests of the movement. In the early spring of 1943, the Mandate authorities uncovered a significant portion of the intricate Zionist smuggling network.[41] Two British soldiers were implicated in the affair, and their subsequent trial revealed the possible involvement of Ben Gurion, the Histadrut, and the ha-Poel Workers' Sports Organization). All this caused the defense attorney to remark that the soldiers had become ensnared in "an organization so powerful and so ruthless that once its tentacles had enclosed on them, there was virtually no escape." [42] One must temper this statement with the realization that it was spoken by a person charged with the defense of the soldiers. However, it is impossible to disregard it totally in the light of the whole story of the diplomacy and operations of political Zionism.

The ultimate result of Zionist activism in Palestine during the war years was the erection of such a barrier between the Jewish Agency and the Mandate authorities that the former opposed virtually any act by the latter which stood in the way of the fulfillment of the Biltmore Program.[43] By the end of the war, the Agency had acquired the attributes of an independent government. In the words of Arthur Koestler: ". . . the Jewish Agency, by force of circumstances, had de-

75

veloped into a shadow Government, a state within the State. It controlled the Jewish economic sector of the country, it had its own hospitals and social services, it ran its own schools, its own intelligence service with virtually all Jewish Government officials as voluntary informers, and controlled its own para-military organization, the famous Haganah, nucleus of the future Army of Israel." [44] A nascent Israel was already in existence.

CHAPTER VIII

THE ZIONIST SEARCH FOR AMERICAN SUPPORT

The Zionists had two primary reasons for devoting special attention to the United States during the war period. First, in their difficulties with Great Britain over the 1939 White Paper, they came to feel that if American opposition to the White Paper could be developed, a significant pressure could be brought to bear on the British.[1] This was especially true during the early part of the war, since the United States was still only a potential ally and the British were anxious to maintain perfect harmony in the relations between the two countries. The second main purpose for the increased Zionist interest in the United States was to replace Great Britain with America as the mainspring of Gentile support. The imperial power of Britain seemed on the decline,[2] and if America entered the war, it was entirely possible that she would emerge from the conflict as the leader of the West. If this should happen, as in fact it did, it would be absolutely essential for Zionism to possess the advantage of American support. Beyond this, Zionism's new policy of imminent statehood in the post-war period implied a struggle against the British, since statehood precluded any continuation of the Mandate. The old era of cooperation with the British had come to an end, and the issue of the White Paper went a step further and made Britain a potential enemy.

It was with these considerations that the Zionists devoted

great efforts to make America the center of Gentile support during the war, for after the defeat of the Axis, that support would have to be immediately forthcoming if the Biltmore Program were to be fulfilled. The Zionists went about their task on three different levels to insure ultimate success. They sought to win to their cause the American people, the Congress, and the Administration.

Winning the People

The American Emergency Committee for Zionist Affairs, later the American Zionist Emergency Council, was charged with the task of propagandizing the Zionist cause in America.[3] The Committee was organized for this purpose into 76 state and regional branches, with 380 committees on the local level.[4] In April, 1941, the Emergency Committee assisted in the formation of the American Palestine Committee, the aim of which was to enlist the support of American Christians.[5] A related organization, known as the Christian Council on Palestine, was subsequently created to develop a favorable attitude toward Zionism among clergymen.[6] This approach to the American public was made easier by the prevalence of Protestant opinion which had been conditioned by close study and literal interpretation of the Old Testament, a circumstance which the Zionists carefully exploited.[7] As has already been pointed out, however, political Zionism may have little validity from a Christian point of view.

Aside from grooming the support of clergymen and Church groups, the Zionists also sought the cooperation of journalists and persons in public service.[8] This groundwork was followed by an extensive campaign. In 1943, this campaign got into full swing in an endeavor to ". . . inject Zionism's political-nationalism into every crevice of the American scene." [9] As in Britain, the Zionist propaganda in America was overtly designed to engender opposition to the 1939 White Paper, but sought simultaneously to promote backing of Zionism's new policy—the establishment of Jewish statehood.[10] This added provision was frequently endorsed unwittingly, and many who would have otherwise hesitated to support a program of imminent statehood were thus committed to such a stand without realizing it.[11] Once again, the combination of Zionist ingenuity and the general ignorance of Zionism's implications on the part of Christians resulted in the development of significant Gentile support for Zionism.

The Zionist propaganda campaign was an ultimate success. As a result of it, 33 state legislatures, the C.I.O., and the A.F. of L. passed resolutions favoring Zionism.[12] Later, both houses of Congress introduced similar resolutions, and in the 1944 election campaign, the two major political parties adopted pro-Zionist planks. These events will be discussed later, but it is significant to note here that the Zionist propaganda campaign did much to encourage these resolutions. As one example, the introduction of the resolutions in Congress was followed by a deluge of telegrams to Senators and Representatives, urging them to support the resolutions,[13] an event which may reflect the effectiveness of Zionism's public relations.

While the Zionists were making these strides in the influencing of American Gentile opinion, they did not neglect the Jews. American Jewry was assimilationist by tradition.[14] Even in 1943, the total number of American Jews affiliated with Zionism amounted to less than five per cent of the country's Jewish population.[15] This posed a serious problem for the Zionists, and the third point of the Herzlian program —the development of Jewish support—was called into action. To contend with the challenge, the Palestine Executive sent propaganda officers known as *shlichim* to America to undertake the task of convincing American Jewry that political Zionism was the only solution to the crisis then facing world Jewry.[16]

The main argument the Zionists used to draw American Jewry into the movement was to point up the need of the oppressed Jews of Europe for asylum. The tragic migrations of these victims of Hitler's anti-Semitism were presented as proof of the underlying need and desire of world Jewry to build its own nationality.[17] Thus, they employed the general sympathy of all people of good will in selling the idea of Jewish statehood. To the Zionists, asylum was not the real issue—rather it was the current need of Jews for asylum that they employed to justify the establishment of a Jewish state in Palestine. In the post-war period, the Zionists showed their true interests in this matter by withholding their support from a program developed by Roosevelt to provide new homes for Jewish refugees in the Diaspora.[18]

In its eventual outcome, the Zionist attempt to win American Jewry was as successful as the campaign to win the American Gentile public. By the end of the war, the ranks of American Zionism were nearly doubled,[19] while in the post-war period it became next to impossible for a Jew to oppose Zionism and retain the respect of his fellow Jews. In the fall of 1943, the Zionists succeeded in committing the American Jewish Conference, a gathering of all factions of American Jewry, to an endorsement of the Biltmore Program.[20] The non-Zionist American Jewish Committee and a number of other Jewish organizations with similar views objected to this endeavor to make American Jewry at large a Zionist dependency. Even though the Committee had in the past provided a large portion of the non-Zionist membership of the Jewish Agency,[21] they were forthwith ostracized by the Zionists. Rabbi Wise, co-chairman of the Emergency Council, and Mr. Henry Monsky, President of B'nai Brith, accused the American Jewish Committee of trying to divide American Jewry, while others insisted that they were acting against the interests of American Jews.[22] These denunciations were followed by the resignation of all Zionists from the Committee, thereby securing its isolation, just as had been the case with the non-Zionists in Britain. During all of this, the once-championed principles of the Jewish Agency[23] were obscured and the doctrine of minority voice and open opposition was all but forgotten. It was a Zionist landslide, and American Jewry was won.

Winning the Congress

While the Zionists were seeking to win the American public to the principle of Jewish statehood, the groundwork was laid for the eventual conversion of the United States Congress to the Zionist cause. The first step, which has already been mentioned, was the enrollment of 67 Senators and 143 Representatives in the American Palestine Committee. In December of 1942, Congress again demonstrated its susceptibility to Zionist propaganda when one-third of the Senate joined one and a half thousand other public figures in signing a Revisionist proclamation demanding the creation of a Jewish Army.[24]

These initial successes with Congressmen led the Zionists to seek further support from the American Legislative Branch. What was needed now was a Congressional declaration backing the Biltmore Program. On October 6, 1943, a group of 500 rabbis arrived at the Capitol and presented Zionist demands to Vice-President Wallace.[25] This was supplemented by Zionist lobbying, [26] and in January, 1944, resolutions endorsing the Biltmore Program were introduced in both houses of Congress.[27] The resolutions were subsequently shelved on the advice of the Chief of Staff, General Marshall,

81

who felt that their passage would be detrimental to the Allied war effort.[28] Nevertheless, it is little short of amazing that the United States came so close to committing itself officially to a movement of international consequence, the history and implications of which were barely known or understood. This was the result of just three years of Zionist concentration in America.

The story of the handling of the proposed resolution favoring Zionism in the House of Representatives affords a good insight into the Zionists' success with Congress. When the resolution was introduced into that body, it was referred to the Committee on Foreign Affairs, the chairman of which was Sol Bloom, a representative from New York and a Zionist. Bloom hoped at first that the resolution would find approval without the necessity of a hearing.[29] At this point, however, the American Council for Judaism, an anti-Zionist Jewish organization, pressed for hearings, which were subsequently held.[30] This is reminiscent of the role played by British non-Zionist Jews during the First World War, when the original Zionist draft of the Balfour Declaration was revised at their insistence to include recognition of the rights of the non-Jewish community of Palestine and of Jews in the Diaspora.

When the House hearings got under way, Sol Bloom presented the members of the Committee with a pamphlet he had prepared for the purpose of instructing them on all relevant matters connected with the resolution. Actually, however, the booklet was primarily devoted to summarizing the Zionist position on Palestine, and concluded with a memorandum of the Jewish Agency vilifying the 1939 White Paper.[31] It did not even contain a report from the State Department, which is not short of surprising inasmuch as the resolution up for consideration involved a significant development in American foreign policy, the handling of which is specifically assigned to the State Department by the President. One is forced also to note that Bloom appeared to employ his position as chairman of the Committee to guide the discussion in such a way as to avoid embarrassment to Zionism.[32]

Although nothing came of the resolutions before the Congress at this time, the Zionists compensated for the temporary setback at the national conventions the following summer. This combined effect of Zionist attempts to influence the public and to recruit members of Congress resulted in the adoption by both party conventions of pro-Zionist planks.[33] By this time, the Zionists had been so successful in identifying American Jewry with their cause in the minds of Gentiles and many Jews that neither party felt it could fail to endorse Zionism and hope to find any support from the Jewish electorate. Once the elections were over, Sol Bloom took the responsibility for reminding the Congressmen of their party platform and campaign pledges, a task he accomplished by means of a pamphlet which he had printed by the Government Printing Office.[34] In effect, the American Congress was won, and there could be no turning back. The Zionists had virtually committed the United States to their cause by ". . . sheer number of resolutions. . . ."[35]

Winning the Administration

The task of winning the support of the American Administration to the Zionist cause was assigned during the war years to Zionism's past master at diplomacy on the very highest levels of government, Dr. Weizmann. During the war, Weizmann made three trips to the United States, and on each occasion he devoted considerable time and energy to obtaining the Administration's commitment to Zionism and the principles of the Biltmore Program. His first interview with Roosevelt was in February, 1940, at which time he tried to sound out the President on the possibilities of an official American stand opposing the MacDonald White Paper.[36] The caution of this approach—the subject of statehood was carefully avoided by Weizmann—failed, however, to evoke more than friendly but non-committal response from the President. It was perhaps at this first encounter that Weizmann became aware of Roosevelt's unique political savoir faire, and time was to prove that the President, though never inimical to Zionism, always hesitated to grant it special favor, since he believed there was wisdom in seeking a joint Arab-Zionist solution to the problem of Palestine.

Weizmann travelled to America again in the spring of 1941. This time he went at the request of the British Government to look into the then current trend of anti-British propaganda in the United States.[37] This situation is reminiscent of the First World War period, when the Zionists offered to assist the British war effort by rallying world Jewry—and American Jews in particular—behind the Allied cause. Weizmann may not have asked anything in exchange for this service in 1941, but there is no question that the Zionist offer during the First World War was merely their part of a bargain, in which the British obligation was to support the Zionist cause.

During the 1941 visit, Weizmann conversed with Sumner Welles, who was already favorably disposed toward Zionism, and other top government officials. As in his dealings with the British Government, however, he found that the lower echelons refused to be won over to the Zionist cause.[38] On this level were the men who had served and specialized in the Middle East, and just as the British commissions had balked at Zionism's insistence that its own demands receive exclusive attention, so the American State Department officials and others charged with United States policy in the

84

Middle East as a whole would not regard Zionism's interests as isolated or special. But just as the policies suggested by British commissions had been reversed in London, so, too, could the opinions of American experts on the Middle East be reversed in Washington. Weizmann, therefore, continued to concentrate on the top levels, where decisions from below could easily be reversed.

Early in 1942, Weizmann was requested by Roosevelt to come to the United States to help out on the development of synthetic rubber. As a result of this request, Weizmann came once again to America in April, 1942, and remained until July of the following year. During this period, he devoted his time not only to chemistry, but also to questioning leading Americans on what lines of support Zionism could expect from the United States.[39] Before leaving, he had another interview with Roosevelt in the presence of Sumner Welles.[40] At this meeting, Roosevelt once again avoided positive commitment to Zionism, but expressed his general sympathy with the movement, while Welles tried to evoke a more favorable response from the President by underwriting the idea of Jewish statehood and suggesting American financial support in the matter of establishing that statehood. Roosevelt had already begun to lean toward the idea of an Arab-Jewish settlement of the Palestine problem and suggested such a course of action at this meeting. Weizmann countered, however, by stating that if the establishment of the Jewish National Home depended on Arab consent, it would never be established. His alternate suggestion was that Great Britain and the United States take a strong stand behind the establishment of the Home, or State, and thus force the Arabs to acquiesce in the face of overwhelming power, just as they had been forced to acquiesce to the Balfour Declaration and its consequences by British might.[41]

In spite of Weizmann's suggestions, Roosevelt went ahead

with his plan to include the Arabs in the ultimate settlement of the question of Palestine. When it became known that he was seeking Ibn Sa'ud's cooperation in this matter, the American Zionists took the offensive. On August 18, 1943, Emmanuel Celler, a pro-Zionist Congressman from New York, threatened the President with a Congressional investigation if action were not taken to prevent the State Department from continuing its opposition to Zionism.[42] This was an indirect way of threatening the President himself. It was not until somewhat later, however, that the Zionists were able to make any real progress with Roosevelt.

At the time of the suspension of action on the proposed Congressional resolutions endorsing Jewish statehood, Rabbis Wise and Silver, co-chairmen of the American Zionist Emergency Council, were successful in getting Roosevelt to make a statement intimating American opposition to the 1939 White Paper. The actual wording of the statement, which Wise and Silver were authorized to forward to the press, was so carefully couched that in essence it made no real commitment to Zionism.[43] In reference to the White Paper, the President said that the United States Government had never given its approval of that policy. But this did not announce any active American opposition to the White Paper, and furthermore, the Mandate was in no way the charge or concern of the United States. The President's further remarks were equally evasive: he was glad the doors of Palestine were now open and hoped justice would be done to those who sought a Jewish National Home. Nevertheless, the Zionists could use even this half-hearted support of their cause by interpreting it in such a manner as to give the American public the idea that their Chief Executive was fully behind the principles of the Biltmore Program. The statement fit well into the election year program of the Zionists, and had it not been an election year, one may speculate as to whether

Wise and Silver would have gotten this much of an endorsement.

A year later—on March 16, 1945—Wise tried to provoke a further statement by the President.[44] It was at this time that Zionist agitation had been aroused over Roosevelt's meeting with Ibn Sa'ud following the Yalta Conference. Nevertheless, Roosevelt who was apparently convinced at this point of the necessity of an Arab-Jewish rapprochement on Palestine, refused to go any further than he had the previous year and stated simply that he had not changed his position on Zionism.

Even though the Zionists were by and large unsuccessful in their dealings with Roosevelt, they initiated during his administration a tradition of seeking to influence American policy on the Middle East through the White House.[45] And during the presidency of Truman, this tactic was to bring handsome and enduring rewards. For with the advent of Truman, the Administration joined the Congress and the public to become a new prize in the Zionist struggle for Jewish statehood.

CHAPTER IX

THE MAKING OF MODERN ISRAEL

The Zionists and the Truman Administration

With the conclusion of World War II, the Zionists were faced with the crucial task of bringing about the implementation of the Biltmore Program. Having suffered an initial disappointment with the failure of the Yalta Conference to deal substantially with the Palestine question,[1] they turned primarily to the United States for Gentile support in the matter of achieving Jewish statehood. Zionism's hour of ultimate success or failure had come, but the preparatory work accomplished in America during the war provided the needed advantages to insure victory.

Following the death of Roosevelt, the Zionists moved swiftly to make themselves and their platform known to the new President. Only a few days after Truman had been sworn in, he was visited by Rabbi Wise. Edward Stettinius, then Secretary of State, had already briefed the new President on Roosevelt's Palestine policy and cautioned him that Zionist leaders would try to obtain his commitment to the Zionist program of unlimited immigration and the establishment of a Jewish state.[2] Time was to prove, however, that Wise's visit to Truman was only the beginning of Zionism's ultimate conversion of the Administration to its cause.

The story of Truman's increasing willingness to be drawn

into the service of Zionism becomes clearer in the light of several factors. First, as a liberal, he was spontaneously enthusiastic about anything which seemed to be doing a service for Jews or any other minority. This is one of the keys to understanding Gentile Zionism, though ironically enough, the liberal idea logically aims at assimilation, while Zionism is based on the premise that assimilation is impossible. Thus, to endorse Zionism is, in a sense, to admit the failure of the West to cope with its own racial prejudice.

Linked to this liberal basis of Truman's pro-Zionist tendencies was his natural sympathy for the Jewish refugees of Europe.[3] Here again, he allowed the Zionists to equate in his mind the salvation of the refugees with the fulfillment of the Zionist program. This was a result of the Zionists' wartime publicity campaign, which had spread the notion that Zionism was the only solution to the Jewish refugee problem. Few stopped to think whether the existence of Jewish refugees necessarily justified Zionism and the premises upon which it rests.

A further explanation of Truman's pro-Zionist leaning was his apparent confusion as to the meaning of Wilsonian principles and their application to Middle East realities. In his memoirs, Truman states that he had always felt that the Balfour Declaration went hand-in-hand with the Wilsonian doctrine of self-determination.[4] Though one does not question the sincerity of the President in this expression of sympathy with the two doctrines, one is equally forced to note the naivete of Truman in this matter. For the doctrines are not only unrelated to each other, but actually contradictory. The self-determination principle, if applied to Palestine, would have precluded the possibility of building up a Jewish state in that country, since the great majority of the inhabitants were non-Jewish at the time the Fourteen Points were proclaimed by Wilson. And furthermore, critics of Zionism have pointed to the events leading up to the creation of Israel as a marked violation of the principle of self-determination, and this they have done with argument not lacking in logic. Therefore, it seems evident that Truman, however sincere and humane his motives, appeared to lack clear understanding of the principles involved. This is not to question his right to support the creation of Jewish statehood, but to deny his logic in justifying it by the doctrine of self-determination.

In the summer of 1945, the influence of the Zionists over Truman became apparent.[5] On August 31, the President took his first positive action on behalf of Zionism by asking Prime Minister Attlee of Great Britain to admit 100,000 Jewish refugees into Palestine.[6] Byrnes, who was then Secretary of State, subsequently became concerned over the reaction to the Truman request in the Arab Middle East. He therefore announced on October 18th, that the United States Government ". . . would not support a final decision which in its opinion would affect the basic situation in Palestine without full consultation of both Jews and Arabs."[7] In effect, this was a reassertion of the Roosevelt doctrine on Palestine, of which Joseph Grew had informed Truman earlier in the year.[8]

In response to Truman's request that 100,000 Jews be allowed into Palestine, Attlee reminded the President of the commitments which had been made to the Arab peoples. Later, the British Government suggested the creation of an Anglo-American commission to study the Palestine situation and to recommend what appropriate actions should be taken.[9] The story of the Anglo-American Committee of Inquiry will be told later, but it should be noted here that of the various recommendations it made, Truman selected those favorable to Zionism for his public praise and approval.[10] Among these was Truman's own suggestion that

90

100,000 Jews be admitted to Palestine, and when it appeared as a Committee recommendation, the President announced that the United States would assume the financial responsibility of transporting the refugees to Palestine.[11]

While Truman was trying to get the British to adopt a softer line in the matter of immigration, the Zionists were, in his words, making his task more difficult by seeking American support of Jewish statehood.[12] On October 30, 1945, the President received a wire from Rabbis Wise and Silver, suggesting that the idea of sending another committee to investigate the Palestine situation be abandoned in favor of a policy pronouncement favoring not only the abrogation of the 1939 White Paper and the immediate admission of 100,000 Jews into Palestine, but also calling for the implementation of the intent of the Balfour Declaration.[13] By "intent," of course, all Zionists meant the creation of Jewish statehood, though this is really the intent of Zionism, not of the Balfour Declaration, which safeguarded the non-Jewish community of Palestine.

Truman's difficulty in understanding why the Zionists were impeding his efforts to help them by asking for more than the easing of immigration into Palestine is another indication of his almost naive comprehension of the Zionist movement. Had he made even a cursory study of Zionist operations in America during the war, he would have realized that the Zionists had adopted a firm policy stressing imminent Jewish statehood. He would have seen that their campaign to engender American opposition to the 1939 White Paper and American sympathy for the plight of European Jews was really aimed at selling the idea of a Jewish state in Palestine to the American public, the Congress, and the Administration.

Reflecting on the refugee problem in Europe and the Zionist bid for statehood, Truman confides: "In my own mind, the aims and goals of the Zionists at this stage to set up a Jewish state were secondary to the more immediate problems of finding means to relieve the human misery of the displaced persons." [14] Here again is evidence not only of the President's genuine sincerity and sense of Christian charity as to the refugee problem, but also of his failure to understand Zionism. To political Zionism, the basic aims and goals of the movement are never secondary. This is not to say that the Zionists were not deeply concerned over the plight of European Jews, but that they believe Jewish statehood to be the only true solution to the Jewish problem. [15]

That the Zionists regarded the refugee problem as secondary to the aim of Zionism was brought out during the latter part of the war and again on two occasions after the conclusion of peace. During the war, President Roosevelt became interested in developing a scheme whereby the Jewish refugees of Europe could be settled in welcoming nations throughout the world. Morris L. Ernst was assigned by the President to undertake the preliminary planning of this humanitarian program. Ernst discovered, however, that the work which he regarded as a great project for the salvation of uprooted European Jewry was looked on by the Zionists as an insidious scheme which threatened the fulfillment of Zionism itself. Ernst describes this Zionist reaction, which certainly would have dumbfounded anyone who did not understand Zionism, in the following highly enlightening passage: [16]

> I was amazed and even felt insulted when active Jewish leaders decried, sneered and then attacked me as if I were a traitor. At one dinner party I was openly accused of furthering this plan of freer immigration [of Jews to countries throughout the world] in order to undermine political Zionism. . . . Zionist friends of mine opposed [the Roosevelt program]. . . .

92

> . . . I could see why . . . the leaders of these [Zionist]
> movements should feel that their pet thesis was endangered
> by the generosity and humanity of the F.D.R. program.

On two occasions after the war, the Zionists demonstrated
this same indifference to humanitarian concern for Jewish
displaced persons if that concern did not envision their
settlement in Palestine. When on December 15, 1946, the
General Assembly of the United Nations underwrote the
suggestion that the members of the world organization open
their doors to refugees, the Zionists and other Jews in the
Diaspora whose conversion they had effected, received the
resolution with little welcome.[17] Similarly, when hearings
were held in 1947 on a bill before the House of Representatives in connection with the admission of displaced persons
into the United States, the Zionists showed a marked lack
of enthusiasm.[18] In a word, the Zionists continued to regard
the establishment of Jewish statehood as primary and above
all other considerations. One might almost infer from their
actions that they were interested in the problem of Jewish
refugees largely insofar as it aided the statehood goal of political Zionism.

The year 1946 was a Congressional election year in the
United States, and the Zionists employed this circumstance
to further their cause. In New York State, it was reported
that Dewey was considering the advisability of making a
statement favoring Zionism. Mead and Lehman, who were
running on the Democratic ticket for Senator and Gover-
nor, respectively, immediately proceeded to press Truman
for a similar proclamation on behalf of the Democratic Party.
The result of this was a statement by Truman calling once
again for the admission of 100,000 Jews into Palestine, and
thus the Administration, as well as both parties, became further committed to the support of Zionism.[19] In the following

93

year, the President was to express regret that he committed himself to Zionism so decisively when he originally made his statement about the 100,000 Jewish refugees in 1945.[20] However, in 1946, when the Zionists were ". . . injecting vigorous and active propaganda to force the President's hand with reference to the immediate immigration of Jews into Palestine . . . ," [21] there was no possibility for him to turn back. And in 1947, his expression of regret was little more than ineffectual hindsight, for already the Zionists had won the Administration and were on the brink of statehood.

The Zionists and the Labor Government in Britain

In spite of its pro-Zionist resolutions during the war, the Labor Party adopted a firmer attitude toward Zionism when it came to power in 1945. The first sign of this policy was Prime Minister Attlee's refusal to give spontaneous sanction to the Truman proposal that 100,000 Jewish refugees be allowed immediate entry into Palestine. It was also at this time that the new Foreign Minister, Ernest Bevin, announced that immigration into Palestine would be restricted to 1,500 per month.[22] Later, Weizmann was in touch with Bevin in connection with the small number of immigration certificates being issued.[23] In contempt, the Zionists had refused any certificates at all, preferring to accept nothing short of their full demands. Bevin challenged Weizmann on this action, exclaiming, "Are you trying to force my hand? If you want a fight you can have it!" [24] Now that the Labor Party had been charged with the responsibility of the Mandate and of Britain's relations with the Middle East as a whole, it had to consider the interests of the non-Jewish community of Palestine as well as those of the Zionists, a balanced approach which earned Bevin the severe disapproval of Weizmann.

94

What the Zionists appeared to be actually seeking was the establishment of policies partisan to their goal. This is essentially what Weizmann had sought with Roosevelt at an earlier date.[25] With the Labor Party, the Zionists never achieved this, just as they had not really achieved it with Roosevelt. However, this did not really matter, for as the Truman Administration became gradually committed to the Zionist cause, Zionism achieved the necessary Gentile support to reach its goal of Jewish statehood.

Through the United States, the Zionists exerted an increasing pressure on Britain's Labor Government. Following a statement opposing the admission of 100,000 Jews into Palestine made by Bevin in June, 1946, the two Senators from New York protested directly to the British Foreign Secretary, while Dr. Silver enjoined American citizens to question their Congressmen as to the advisability of making a loan to Britain.[26] It was at this time that Congress was considering a loan of $3,750,000,000 to the United Kingdom,[27] and the attempt of the Zionists to pressure the British Government by threatening to work actively against the passage of the bill was extremely effective in forcing the British to water down their Arab policies and assume a position more favorable to the Zionists.[28] Later, when the British gave up in Palestine, it was again the United States which won the day for Zionism when the battle for partition was fought out in the United Nations. As a result, the setbacks endured by the Zionists in Great Britain were compensated for by their success in America, and thus ultimate victory became a matter of course.

Prime Minister Attlee's proposal that an Anglo-American investigation precede any definitive decision on the Palestine problem led to the creation of the Anglo-American Committee of Inquiry. The Committee was composed of six Americans and six Britishers, who studied the problem until

April of 1946. The Truman Administration has often been accused of stacking this Committee with pro-Zionists, and though this accusation is difficult to substantiate, it is noteworthy that of the American members, James G. MacDonald is today in the employ of the Zionist Organization of America and Bartley Crum has authored a book[29] and made numerous public statements leaving no doubt of his pro-Zionist proclivity.

The final recommendations of the Committee pleased neither the Zionists nor the Arabs.[30] On the one hand, the Truman proposal that 100,000 Jewish refugees be admitted to Palestine was endorsed; on the other, the exclusive right of either the Arabs or the Jews to establish statehood in the country was denied.[31] Subsequently, special British and American committees met in London to discuss the implementation of the recommendations made by the Anglo-American Committee of Inquiry. These talks resulted in the Morrison-Grady Plan, an impractical scheme for the cantonization of Palestine under British supervision.[32] This plan was rejected by both Arabs and Jews, and thus the whole undertaking which had begun with the appointment of the Committee of Inquiry was doomed to failure.

Commenting on this outcome, Bevin made several penetrating and thought-provoking comments in the House of Commons. He complained that he could have arrived at an Arab-Jewish settlement of the Palestine question had President Truman not insisted on the political expediency to his party of further statements favoring the admission of 100,000 Jews into Palestine. "In international affairs," he exclaimed, "I cannot settle things if my problem is made the subject of local elections." [33] He argued further that the problem of Jewish refugees could be settled by their immigration to Palestine if this were handled on a humanitarian instead of a political level. "Unfortunately," he said, "that is not the

96

position. From the Zionist point of view, the 100,000 is only a beginning, and the Jewish Agency talk in terms of millions." [34] He also expressed the feeling that there was no moral basis on which to support the establishment of a Jewish majority in what had theretofore been a country inhabited by a Jewish minority.[35] He saw clearly the difference between the humanitarian problem of the refugees and the political problem of Zionism, and he did not permit himself to forget that the Balfour Declaration did not make pledges only to the Zionists.

For such clear insight into the complex problem of Palestine, Bevin incurred the wrath of Zionism, just as in 1946 his insistence that there was a distinction between Zionism and Jewry aroused a storm of Zionist protest.[36] That there is a difference cannot be questioned in the light of honest investigation, but the program of Herzl had always aimed at obscuring that distinction. It was really Bevin's clarity that the Zionists could not tolerate. They also easily forgot that Weizmann himself had admitted before the Anglo-American Committee of Inquiry that the establishment of a Jewish state in Palestine would be unjust to the Arabs, and had pleaded that Zionism's fulfillment involved the lesser injustice.[37] But all this was academic. It was Zionism's persistent practicality which carried the day.

The Labor Party was challenged by the Zionists not only in Britain, but also in Palestine. The Zionist attempt to negate the policy of the 1939 White Paper through activist resistance during the war continued and expanded after the conclusion of hostilities. In the post-war period, Jewish terrorism became more closely linked to the Zionist leadership, while the promotion of illegal immigration was established as the policy of the Jewish community.

In September, 1945, the Zionist leadership in Palestine and London drew up plans to force Britain's hand by means

97

of a specially designed terrorist campaign. At its inception, the scheme was outlined in these words by a member of the Jewish Agency Executive in Palestine:[38]

> It has also been suggested that we cause one serious incident. We would then publish a declaration to the effect that it is only a warning and an indication of much more serious incidents that would threaten the safety of all British interests in the country, should the Government decide against us. . . . The Stern Group have expressed their willingness to join us completely on the basis of our programme of activity. This time the intention seems serious. If there is such a union we may assume that we can prevent independent action by the IZL [Irgun Zvai Leumi].

This blueprint of an activist program based on cooperation between the Zionist leadership and the terrorist organizations whose violence they had always deprecated was soon transmitted into action. On the last day of October, the members of an elite Jewish commando group known as the Palmach blew up the railways in scores of places, while the Irgun Zvai Leumi and the Stern Group attacked the Lydda rail yards and the Haifa refinery, respectively.[39] This outburst of organized violence served to frustrate the British authorities in Palestine and to inaugurate a campaign of terror which ultimately drove Britain to abandon the Mandate and turn the Palestine problem over to the United Nations.

That the post-war Jewish terrorism was not only highly organized but coordinated by the Zionist leadership seems evident from the facts of the above incidents as they are known and also through the evidence presented by a British White Paper (not the 1939 White Paper) which linked the Zionist leaders of Palestinian Jewry to the terrorists.[40] Yet the leaders of the Zionist movement continued to insist that they had nothing to do with the terrorists and abjured the

98

acts of violence committed by Jews in Palestine. Weizmann declared his opposition to Jewish activism, but one is given cause to conjecture on his actual stand in this matter in the light of evidence pointing to Weizmann's implication in the outburst of October 31, 1945.[41]

In the post-war period, Zionist activism was concerned as much with the promotion of illegal immigration as it was with terrorism. Following Bevin's announcement that immigration into Palestine would be restricted to 1,500 monthly, the whole Zionist machinery in Palestine declared its intention to sponsor illegal immigration on a large scale. The Assembly, the Inner General Council, and the Jewish Agency Executive all endorsed this position.[42] This reaffirmed a policy which had been inaugurated during the war, but the endorsement of that policy in 1945 turned the standing friction over immigration into a bitter struggle which demanded resolution.

The Zionist strategy in the matter of post-war illegal immigration was far from haphazard. It was in all respects carefully planned and adroitly maneuvered. Behind the apparently spontaneous flow of Jews from Europe to Palestine was a network of Zionist agents, who not only helped to stimulate the migration[43] but also to facilitate it. An intelligence report of the American Third Army reveals the existence in the immediate post-war period of an underground Zionist organization which sponsored the infiltration of 2,000 Jews weekly into the American zone of occupation.[44] The Zionist agents who made up this organization, some of whom were Jews serving in the Allied armies, then arranged for the migrating Jews to be conducted to the Mediterranean coast via organized escape routes.[45] Once on the coast, they would be embarked on ships chartered by the Zionists and transported to Palestine. The British Government reported further that this underground railway was supplied with food and other necessities through diversion of UNRRA materiel.[46]

The Zionists maintained that the flow of Jews from Europe to Palestine was entirely spontaneous and unorganized. Yet there are a number of factors to indicate that this was not precisely the case. First, the very fact that the Zionists went out of their way to boycott and discourage the resettlement of Jewish refugees in the Diaspora is indication of their fear that the majority of Europe's Jewish refugees might not choose Palestine over havens elsewhere in the world. Secondly, most of the refugees chosen by the Zionists for transport to Palestine via the underground railway were young men and women who could play an active role in assisting the Zionist struggle for statehood.[47] This is another indication that the movement's political requirements dominated humanitarian concerns, although the humanitarian aspects were stressed before the world. Thirdly, when the Third Army report on the Zionist underground was revealed by Lt. Gen. Sir Frederick Morgan, chief of UNRRA in Germany, early in 1946, Herbert Lehman, a pro-Zionist and Director-General of UNRRA, relieved Morgan of his post on the charge of anti-Semitism.[48] Morgan was later reinstated, but this incident indicates the defensiveness of Zionism on this matter and thereby serves to suggest not only the greater likelihood of the underground's existence, but also that the Zionists sought to conceal it from a public for whom they were painting a very different picture of their movement and the manner in which it operated. Fourthly, that Jewish immigration to Palestine was not an entirely spontaneous phenomenon is further suggested by the fact that once the flow of illegal immigrants met with effective British opposition, the Zionists in England initiated a drive to raise 100,000 pounds sterling for the purpose of facilitating the passage of Jews to Palestine.[49]

100

In conclusion, therefore, it may be stated that the available evidence points to the post-war exodus of Jews from Europe to Palestine as a phenomenon largely contrived by Zionists.[50] The Zionist Organization not only resolved to sponsor illegal immigration, but actually stimulated, organized, and financed it. The purpose, which was to prepare for an imminent *de facto* assertion of statehood and to render the Mandate unworkable, was soon realized, and the final battle was fought out in the United Nations with the support of the United States.

The United Nations and Partition

The Zionist war of attrition against the Mandate authorities was ultimately victorious, for the British admitted their failure as mandatory in 1947, and on April 2nd of that year, Britain requested the United Nations to place the question of Palestine on their agenda.[51] Britain could no longer cope with a situation which in the post-war period was made intolerable by the Zionists. Thus, the Zionists succeeded in placing the problem of Palestine before the world community in such a manner that it posed a choice. Either the Mandate was to be continued or some form of independence was to be granted the peoples of Palestine. This was a major step, since it raised the question of nationalism in Palestine, a condition which had not theretofore been presented for serious consideration. With this question on the agenda of the United Nations, the only further step to be taken by the Zionists was to insure that the United Nations approve the principle of independence for Palestine and then sanction the creation of a Jewish state in all or part of Palestine.

Once the question of Palestine was placed on the agenda of the United Nations, a special committee was formed to investigate the Palestine situation and to make recommendations.[52] This Committee's final recommendation fulfilled the second vital need of Zionist policy at this crucial moment in the history of the movement: the principle of independence was endorsed. There was, however, disagreement as to the nature of that independence. Seven of the committee members supported the thesis that the Jewish minority of Palestine should be granted control of the country, while three others thought control should be vested equally in the hands of Jews and Arabs. One had no opinion on the matter at all, and the seven remaining members proposed that Palestine be divided into three parts, consisting of an Arab state, a Jewish state, and an internationalized zone in the Jerusalem area.

In spite of the impracticality of this plan, the Zionists saw in it the seeds of their third diplomatic requirement: recognition of the principle of Jewish statehood. They therefore accepted the concept of partition, and the struggle in the United Nations narrowed on this issue. Though the Zionists were disappointed that they had not been awarded all of Palestine, they recognized the significance of reducing the United Nations inquiry into the Palestine situation to a debate on whether a Jewish state was or was not to be constructed in at least part of Palestine. This left only one task—to insure that the world organization endorse partition.

On October 11, 1947, the United States delegation at the United Nations gave its formal backing to the plan for the partition of Palestine. It did so on the orders of President Truman.[53] Thus, the great effort the Zionists had exerted in their attempt to enlist the support of the President reaped further reward. With the support of the United States, the Zionists had won half the battle. American prestige could go far in influencing other nations to join the pro-partition camp.

In November, Weizmann discovered that the American

delegation was seeking to make partition more acceptable to the Arab delegates by offering to include the southern Negev in the projected Arab state.[54] Immediately, the veteran diplomat of Zionism approached the President, and as a result of their conversation, Truman ordered the American delegation to reverse its offer of the southern Negev to the Arabs. "This decision," Weizmann states in his autobiography, "opened the way to the vote of the General Assembly on November 29. . . ."[55]

Truman's cooperation with Weizmann on the question of the Negev had opened the way for the vote of November 29, but the Zionists still faced the task of insuring enough votes to obtain the two-thirds majority necessary for passage of the partition plan. In the straw votes taken on November 22nd and 26th, less than the required number of votes were pledged to support partition. At this vital hour in Zionism's history, all the movement's political machinery went into action. Haiti, Liberia, the Philippines, China, Ethiopia, and Greece, all of which had shown opposition to partition, became the objects of the most intense Zionist pressure.[56] This pressure was applied indirectly, and in large part, through American channels. The Zionists importuned Congressmen to communicate directly with the governments of the six target countries.[57] The Firestone Tire and Rubber Company, which had a concession in Liberia, was telephoned and urged to persuade the Liberian Government to vote in favor of partition.[58] Under-Secretary of State Robert Lovett attested that ". . . he had never in his life been subject to as much pressure as he had been [during the final stages of the voting]. . . ."[59] Loy Henderson, Director of the State Department's Office of Near Eastern and African Affairs, underwent a similar experience.[60] Herbert Swope and Robert Nathan of the White House staff actively solicited the support of leading officials,[61] and allegedly Justices Frankfurter and Murphy also participated in the Zionist campaign by communicating with the Philippine delegate and urging him to support partition.[62]

These are only a few of the outstanding incidents pointing up the character of the Zionist maneuvers in the United Nations. When the final hour came, all of the six target countries, with the exception of Greece, had agreed either to vote for partition or to abstain,[63] and on November 29th, the General Assembly endorsed the partition of Palestine.

After the historic vote in the United Nations on November 29, 1947, the tactics which the Zionists had employed to secure the outcome they desired came under sharp criticism.[64] This subject remains controversial today. However, significant light is shed by Mr. Truman in his memoirs. In a letter to the President dated November 27, 1947, Dr. Weizmann had asserted that there was no substance to the then current charge in Washington that the Zionists exerted undue pressure on certain United Nations delegations.[65] Mr. Truman's comment on this assertion is as follows:

> The facts were that not only were there pressure movements around the United Nations unlike anything that had been seen there before but that the White House, too, was subjected to a constant barrage. I do not think I ever had as much pressure and propaganda aimed at the White House as I had in this instance. The persistence of a few of the extreme Zionist leaders—actuated by political motives and engaging in political threats—disturbed and annoyed me. Some were even suggesting that we pressure sovereign nations into favorable votes in the General Assembly.[66]

Once partition had been approved, the one remaining task for the Zionists was to secure recognition of the State of Israel. It was the recognition of the United States that was sought above all else. Consequently, "The Jewish pressure on the White House did not diminish in the days following the partition vote in the U.N." [67] As this pressure intensified, the President was forced to refuse audience to Zionist representatives. In spite of the President's instructions, however, Zionists succeeded in getting to him.[68]

In March, 1948, Weizmann made known his desire to see President Truman. In accordance with Truman's instructions, however, Weizmann was denied an interview. Truman then received a call from Mr. Eddie Jacobson, an American Jew and a lifelong friend of the President. Jacobson pleaded with Truman to receive Weizmann, explaining that the Zionist leader was to him the same hero that Andrew Jackson was for the President.[69] Although the timing of Jacobson's visit and his knowledge of the President's refusal to see Weizmann strongly suggested Zionist contrivance, Truman weakened in the face of this unique form of political pressure and agreed to see Dr. Weizmann on March 18th. This interview resulted in the development of a significant rapprochement between the President and the Zionist leader, and on May 14th Truman extended *de facto* recognition to Israel, just eleven minutes after the proclamation of statehood.[70]

Traditionally, the United States has been cautious in recognition of new governments. Therefore, the departure from established American practice in the case of the recognition of Israel serves to show the great success with which the Zionists conducted their operations in the United States. The President's action paved the way for international acceptance of the Israeli state, and James G. MacDonald, whose identification with the Zionists was an established fact,[71] became America's first ambassador to the new nation. Zionism's aim was fulfilled, but it was only fulfilled in part. The third phase was completed with the creation of Israel, but there remained yet a fourth.

EPILOGUE

THE REMAINING TASK
FOR POLITICAL ZIONISM

There is today a prevailing notion that the Zionist movement attained its ultimate fulfillment in the creation of the State of Israel. In actual fact, however, this is not the case, for the aims of political Zionism have been realized only in part.

The original aim of Zionism was to arrive at a satisfactory solution to the problem of anti-Semitism through the development of national status for the Jewish people. For an ethno-religious problem, the Zionists offered a nationalist solution. To this basic principle, they added a specific description of the nation. It was to fall within the historic boundaries of Palestine. By this, they meant not only the Palestine which became a British Mandate, but also Transjordan, southern Lebanon, and Mount Hermon. There is also strong evidence that the Zionists have since 1917 been interested in possession of the Hauran in southern Syria.[1]

At the present time, neither of the above conditions has been fulfilled, for the great majority of world Jewry today does not possess Jewish national status, and the State of Israel does not comprise nearly the area referred to by the Zionists as "historic" Palestine. Thus, Israel represents only an experimental Jewish state. It has failed to bring even a majority[2] of world Jewry within the bounds of Jewish national status, and it is sovereign over less than half of "historic" Palestine, or Eretz Israel (Land of Israel).

This does not mean, however, that the Zionist movement is satisfied with this half-way fulfillment of its traditional aim. On the contrary, that aim abides with the movement, and the Zionists still seek its total fulfillment. It is for this reason that Zionism continues to exist and did not come to a natural dissolution with the creation of Israel. There is still a task to be accomplished, and this task is twofold. First, the Ingathering, or liquidation of the Diaspora, remains to be completed, for until a substantial majority of world Jewry has come to Palestine and accepted Israeli citizenship, Zionism will remain essentially unfulfilled and thwarted in its underlying purpose. Secondly, Zionism is faced with the task of endowing the Israeli state with the boundaries of Eretz Israel, not only for romantic reasons, but to give the state needed economic strength and to provide room for the resettlement of the Jews immigrating from the Diaspora.

Aside from these two tasks, political Zionism must also take the necessary steps to insure the State of Israel's continued existence. To do this, the Zionists have sought the economic and political support of Gentile nations and of Jews in the Diaspora. Thus, if we view the present task now facing political Zionism in historical perspective, we find that the movement's basic aims and policy requirements are not substantially different from what they were in the days of Herzl. The three-point program remains indigenous to the movement: there is still an essential need to concentrate on building the nation, gathering the support and allegiance of world Jewry, and enlisting the help of Gentile nations. Let us examine each of these areas of concentration in their current setting.

The territorial ambitions of Zionism are not a matter of conjecture: throughout the history of the movement these ambitions have been clearly and unmistakably expressed. The Memorandum of the Zionist Organization to the Supreme Council at the Paris Peace Conference in 1919 proposed the inclusion within Palestine of Transjordan and intimated that Mount Hermon and southern Lebanon should also be added to Palestine.[3] The aim behind this proposal was to enable the Balfour Declaration to apply to these areas, thus opening them to Jewish immigration, a condition the Zionists would not have sought had they considered them outside the boundaries of Eretz Israel. When the Churchill White Paper of 1922 definitively excluded Transjordan from Palestine, the Zionists considered it a serious loss to their cause. Weizmann remarks in his autobiography: "The Churchill White Paper was regarded by us as a serious whittling down of the Balfour Declaration. It detached trans-Jordan from the area of Zionist operation. . . ."[4] Weizmann also revealed Zionism's interest in southern Lebanon when he sought French agreement to the inclusion of this region within the boundaries of Palestine in the early 1920's.[5]

Since the establishment of Israel, the Zionists have been more careful to conceal the full extent of their territorial ambitions. Nevertheless, occasional frankness on the matter indicates that the establishment of greater Israel remains a primary objective of the movement. In the Introduction of the *Government Yearbook* of the State of Israel for the year 1952, Mr. Ben Gurion asserts: "It must now be said that it [the State of Israel] has been established in only a portion of the Land of Israel."[6] The *Government Yearbook* for 1955 echoes this view: "The creation of the new State by no means derogates from the scope of historic Eretz Israel."[7] The more extremist parties are even more adamant on the subject of expansion. The Herut and Ahdut Ha'avoda-Poalei Zion Parties are both committed to a policy

108

of expansion, to the establishment of Eretz Israel.[8] It is also possible that the General Zionist Party supports such a policy by implication, since its program asserts that, "The state of Israel does not exist for its own sake but as an instrument for the implementation of the Zionist ideal." Thus, we may clearly discern a continuity of the original idea. In looking at the future through an understanding of the past, we may expect to see this policy guiding the diplomacy of the Zionist movement and of its beachhead, the State of Israel. It is true that there are many Israeli parties which do not advocate expansion, and certainly many of the citizens do not seek a larger Israel. However, it is difficult to support the theory that Zionism has changed its objectives when the continuity of the movement's aims under the direction of a consistent leadership has been so apparent in history. Furthermore, the Ingathering of Jews in the Diaspora, which is widely supported in Zionist circles and championed by Ben Gurion, implies an underlying policy of expansion. For even though some insist that the State of Israel can absorb many more, few would suggest that several millions would manage in an Israel no larger than the present state.

Perhaps the major task currently facing Zionism is that of extending Jewish national status. Should the passage of time fail to bring substantial numbers of Jews to Israel, the movement will begin to lose its vitality. Political Zionism is based on the premise that the one solution to the problem of anti-Semitism is Jewish nationality. This is its essential idea, its ultimate justification. If, however, world Jewry elects to remain in the Diaspora, the whole argument of Zionism will lose its validity, and Israel will remain an experiment. This is a major reason why the Zionists and particularly those in Israel, stress the Ingathering above all other tasks with which they are faced. Ben Gurion asserts that the Ingathering is the essential justification for the establishment and existence of Israel.[9] The Jerusalem Program. which was formulated in 1951 to replace the Basle Program, rests on three principles, two of which are directly concerned with the relationship of world Jewry to Israel.[10] The first principle calls for the "Continuity and Unity of the Jewish People," while the second counsels "The Ingathering of the Exiles in Israel."

These policies reflect the two current methods by which the Zionists are attempting to cope with the problem of a Diaspora which is willing to help but not prepared to become part of Zionism's experimental state. The real aim is embodied in the second principle, but since the Diaspora has been apathetic in its response to the call for immigration, the Zionists have vigorously sought to build up a sense of identity with Israel in the minds of Jews throughout the world. Once again, the Zionists have shown their willingness to adopt a policy of gradualism, which was always championed by Weizmann. In an article which appeared in the *Zionist Review* in 1951, this approach to the problem of the Ingathering was reflected in these words: "The Zionist Movement must continue to aim at the liquidation of the Diaspora and must prepare the Jewish people for this process, step by step." [11]

Mr. Ben Gurion has outlined clearly the nature of this important remaining task for political Zionism in an article which appeared in the *Jerusalem Post* in the summer of 1951.[12] He first reminds the Zionists that "Zionism has not yet been fulfilled. . . . the Jewish nation has not yet been gathered inside Israel. . . ." Next, he proceeds to counsel them on the four main duties of a Zionist. The first of these is to promote the Ingathering, while the following three are related to the support and maintenance of the State of Israel as it exists today. Zionists in the Diaspora are impuned to assist the State of Israel ". . . whether the government to

110

which the Jews in question owe allegiance desire it or not."
The solution to this "duplicity," [13] which is necessary because
". . . there can be no Zionism without the fundamental idea
of one nation entity," is the stimulation of identification
with Jewish nationality through the promotion of the Hebrew language, the national tongue of Israel. The next step
is for Zionists to foster the *halutzic* movement, the sponsorship of immigration to Israel. Ben Gurion summarizes these
tasks in the following words:

> Unconditional assistance to the State of Israel, compul-
> sory Hebrew education and the fostering of the halutzic
> movement—these are, to my mind, the three vital conditions
> for the existence of the Zionist Movement and by their
> fulfillment a person shall be known as Zionist. . . .

This formula, then, consists of two fundamental parts:
the promotion of a sense of identification with and duty
toward the Jewish State, and the immigration of Jews to
that state. The first precedes the second and is the means by
which the second may be fulfilled. As the General Zionists
phrase it so perfectly, "The state of Israel does not exist for
its own sake but as an instrument for the implementation of
the Zionist ideal." [14] The core of that ideal is the imposition
of Jewish nationality on Jews everywhere, and thus the Ingathering is first and foremost among the tasks facing political Zionism today.[15]

The final task for political Zionism is the maintenance of
economic and political support for the State of Israel from
Gentile quarters. The fulfillment of this task is centered
primarily in the United States, the most powerful and eco-
nomically solvent country in the Western world. It is not
necessary to analyze this task in detail, but it is noteworthy
that the United States plays a major role in off-setting the
enormous trade deficit incurred annually by Israel. Also,

111

Israel derives considerable security from the pledges of Gentile nations to uphold the independence and sovereignty of the Jewish State. The maintenance of this Gentile economic and political support is one of the continuous tasks of the movement. Of the fourteen tasks of the Zionist movement attached to the Jerusalem Program of 1951, two are related to the enlisting of Gentile support. The Zionists are enjoined to participate in the "Mobilization of Funds," and in the "Organization of propaganda, and political aid for Israel in cooperation and coordination with the State." [16]

Today, we can look back on sixty years of Zionist diplomacy. In 1897, Theodor Herzl proclaimed the aim of the movement and outlined a three-point program for the fulfillment of that aim. Yet, even after sixty years, the aim and the basic policies remain essentially the same. Since Herzl, the movement has worked methodically and persistently to achieve the realization of its goals. Its leaders have shown great flexibility, pressing for new advantages in the fat years, and waiting patiently in the lean. By this method, they have moved far toward the ultimate realization of their underlying goal. Today their diplomatic task is being carried on in the same manner, and thus we wonder if they are heading toward ultimate success and fulfillment. There are two factors upon which the fate of the movement hangs. The first of these concerns the basic premise of political Zionism: that Jewish nationality is the only solution to the Jewish problem. If the Jews in the Diaspora decide that there is a solution to the Jewish problem in the Diaspora, then Zionism will fail, for its goal will be unattainable. And if the Jews in the Diaspora actually succeed in solving the Jewish problem in the Diaspora, then Zionism will have been proven invalid.

The other factor on which Zionism's future depends is related to the methodology of the movement, the means by

112

which it has accomplished its ends. In the past sixty years, the Zionists have been inclined to adopt almost any means for the fulfillment of their ends. In all fairness, we must admit that they are neither the first nor the last to adopt this view. This is a human tendency, and especially so in movements of zealous national character. However, when the Zionists implanted their state in the midst of another people without first obtaining the permission and cooperation of that people, they ran the risk of engendering a hostile opposition. Today, the Israelis are suffering from this condition, and there is always the possibility that the hostile opposition to which Zionist methodology gave birth may some day make Israel's position in the Middle East untenable.

Only time can tell the role these variable factors will play in Israel's future.

NOTES—CHAPTER I

1 Israel Cohen, *A Short History of Zionism* (London: Frederick Muller, Ltd., 1951), pp. 13-27.

2 Christopher Sykes, *Two Studies in Virtue* (New York: Alfred A. Knopf, 1953), pp. 110-113.

3 *Ibid.*, p. 124.

4 *Ibid.*, pp. 113-114; See also Nahum Goldmann, *The Genius of Herzl and Zionism Today* (Jerusalem: Zionist Executive, 1955), p. 19.

5 Sykes, *op. cit.*, p. 128.

6 James William Parkes, *A History of Palestine from 135 A.D. to Modern Times* (London: Victor Gollancz, Ltd., 1949), p. 267.

7 *Trial and Error, the Autobiography of Chaim Weizmann* (New York: Harper & Brothers, 1949), p. 4.

8 Joseph M. N. Jeffries, *Palestine: the Reality* (London: Longmans, Green & Co., 1939), p. 36.

9 Fannie Fern Andrews, *The Holy Land under Mandate* (Cambridge, Mass.: Houghton Mifflin Co., 1931), I, 303.

10 Parkes, *op. cit.*, p. 267.

11 *Ibid.*, p. 268.

12 Cohen, *op. cit.*, p. 33.

13 Andrews, *op. cit.*, I, 301.

14 Cohen, *op. cit.*, pp. 35-36.

15 Andrews, *op. cit.*, I, 309.

16 Theodor Herzl, *The Jewish State, an Attempt at a Modern Solution of the Jewish Question*, translated by Sylvie D'Avigdor (New York: Scopus Publishing Co., 1943).

17 Andrews, *op. cit.*, I, 311.

18 The ESCO Foundation for Palestine, Inc., *Palestine, a Study of Jewish, Arab and British Policies* (New Haven: Yale University Press, 1947), I, 39.

19 *Ibid.*, I, 40.

20 *Ibid.*

21 See below, p. 107.

22 Jacob C. Hurewitz, *Diplomacy in the Near and Middle East, a Documentary Record* (Princeton, N.J.: D. Van Nostrand Co., Inc., 1956), I (1535-1914), 209.

23 *Ibid.*

24 The ESCO Foundation, *op. cit.*, I, 41.

25 *Ibid.*, I, 42.

26 *Ibid.*, I, 43.

27 *Ibid.*

28 *Ibid.*, I, 44.

29 Nahum Sokolow, *History of Zionism, 1600-1918* (London: Longmans, Green & Co., 1919), I, 295. Herzl had for some time regarded England a potential ally of Zionism. However, the Zionist profession of an identity of interests with the democracies must be tempered by the realization that Zionist diplomats were actively seeking an agreement with the Germans up to the eve of World War I. See Nevill Barbour, *Palestine: Star or Crescent* (New York: Odyssey Press, 1947), pp. 55-56.

30 Sokolow, *op. cit.*, I, 296.

31 *Ibid.*, I, 296-297.

32 Andrews, *op. cit.*, I, 316.

33 *Ibid.*

34 Jeffries, *op. cit.*, p. 38.

35 Andrews, *op. cit.*, I, 321. 78,000 to 88,000 Jews were already there.

36 *Trial and Error*, p. 93.

NOTES—CHAPTER II

1 Sokolow, *op. cit.*, II, 44. English money had financed most Zionist projects.

2 Sykes, *op. cit.*, p. 165.

3 Meyer W. Weisgal (ed.), *Chaim Weizmann, Statesman, Scientist, and Builder of the Jewish Commonwealth* (New York: Dial Press, 1944), p. 131.

4 *Trial and Error*, pp. 121-122.

5 *Ibid.*, p. 122.

6 Weisgal, *op. cit.*, p. 297.

7 M. F. Abcarius, *Palestine through the Fog of Propaganda* (London: Hutchinson & Co., N. D.), p. 44.

8 Sokolow, *op. cit.*, II, 48.

9 Jeffries, *op. cit.*, p. 92.

10 Arnold J. Toynbee, *A Study of History* (London: Oxford University Press, 1954), VIII, 308.

11 *Ibid.*, VIII, 308, footnote.

12 Sykes, *op. cit.*, pp. 149-152.

13 Albertus Pieters, *The Seed of Abraham, a Biblical Study of Israel, the Church, and the Jew* (Grand Rapids, Michigan: Eerdmans Publishing Co., 1950), pp. 132-148. See also, Bishop Lesslie Newbigin, *The Household of God* (New York: Friendship Press, 1954), pp. 38-46.

14 *Trial and Error*, p. 149.

15 The ESCO Foundation, *op. cit.*, I, 80.

16 Jeffries, *op. cit.*, p. 93.

17 *Ibid.*, p. 95.

18 The ESCO Foundation, *op. cit.*, I, 81.

19 *Trial and Error*, pp. 157-158.

20 *Ibid.*, p. 162. Sidebotham was interested in Zionism from the British strategic point of view.

21 Jeffries, *op. cit.*, p. 98.

22 Andrews, *op. cit.*, I, 330.

23 George Antonius, *The Arab Awakening, the Story of the Arab National Movement* (London: Hamish Hamilton, 1945), p. 261; also The ESCO Foundation, *op. cit.,* I, 81.

24 The ESCO Foundation, *op. cit.,* I, 79.

25 Cohen, *op. cit.,* pp. 70-71.

26 Jeffries, *op. cit.,* p. 98.

27 *Ibid.,* p. 99.

28 *Ibid.*

29 See text of the memorandum in The ESCO Foundation, *op. cit.,* I, 84.

30 Sykes, *op. cit.,* p. 176.

31 *Ibid.,* p. 178.

32 *Ibid.*

33 *Ibid.,* pp. 178-179.

34 *Trial and Error,* p. 185.

35 Sykes, *op. cit.,* pp. 181-183.

36 *Ibid.,* pp. 187-188.

37 Andrews, *op. cit.,* I, 330; also, The ESCO Foundation, *op. cit.,* I, 87-89.

38 Full account of the meeting in The ESCO Foundation, *op. cit.,* I, 90-94.

39 Antonius, *op. cit.,* p. 263.

40 The ESCO Foundation, *op. cit.,* I, 92-93.

41 *Ibid.,* I, 94.

42 Jeffries, *op. cit.,* p. 40.

43 Sykes, *op. cit.,* p. 196.

44 *Ibid.,* pp. 198-199.

45 *Ibid.,* pp. 199-200.

46 *Ibid.,* pp. 200-201.

47 See text in Sokolow, *op. cit.,* II, 53.

48 Sykes, *op. cit.,* p. 211.

49 The ESCO Foundation, *op. cit.,* I, 98.

50 See text in Sykes, *op. cit.,* pp. 236-240.

51 *Trial and Error,* p. 179.

52 See text in Hurewitz, *op. cit.,* II (1914-1956), 26.

53 The ESCO Foundation, *op cit.,* I, 105.

54 See text in Hurewitz, *op. cit.,* II, 26.

55 This Jewish concern with the duplicity of national status implied by Zionism has remained an important issue in Jewish circles since this time.

56 The ESCO Foundation, *op. cit.,* I, 113.

57 Sir Charles Webster, "The Art and Practice of Diplomacy," *The Listener,* February 28, 1952, p. 335.

NOTES—CHAPTER III

1 Andrews, *op. cit.,* I, 341-342.

2 See text in Hurewitz, *op. cit.,* II, 45-50; see also *Trial and Error,* pp. 243-244. M. Sylvain Levi, a non-Zionist member of the Zionist Commission, embarrassed the Zionists by reminding the Supreme Council that Zionism implied a threat to the Arab majority of Palestine and a compromise of Jewish national status in the Diaspora.

116

It should also be noted that Congressman Julius Kahn handed to President Wilson on March 4, 1919, a statement signed by prominent American Jews, which voiced opposition to the creation of a Jewish state in Palestine. See text in Morris Jastrow, Jr., *Zionism and the Future of Palestine, the Fallacies and Dangers of Political Zionism* (New York: The Macmillan Company, 1919), pp. 151-159. The statement asserted the belief that the premises contained within it were supported by the majority of American Jews.

3 Andrews, *op. cit.*, I, 355.

4 See text in Raymond P. Stearns, *Pageant of Europe: Sources and Selections from the Renaissance to the Present Day* (New York: Harcourt, Brace & Co., Inc., 1947), pp. 748-749.

5 David Hunter Miller was a member of the British delegation. His published diary of the Peace Conference remains a classic.

6 The ESCO Foundation, *op. cit.*, I, 164-168.

7 *Ibid.*, I, 169.

8 *Ibid.*, I, 170-171.

9 See text in Hurewitz, *op. cit.*, II, 84.

10 The ESCO Foundation, *op. cit.*, I, 172.

11 Milner was a pro-Zionist Cabinet minister.

12 The ESCO Foundation, *op. cit.*, I, 173-174.

13 *Ibid.*, I, 98-99.

14 See text in Hurewitz, *op. cit.*, II, 106-111.

15 Harold W. V. Temperley (ed.), *A History of the Peace Conference of Paris* (London: Henry Frowde & Hodder & Stoughton, 1924), VI, 176. Temperley is the outstanding historian of the Peace Conference.

16 *Trial and Error*, p. 212.

17 Philip Graves, *Palestine, the Land of Three Faiths* (London: Jonathan Cape, 1923), p. 163.

18 *Ibid.*, p. 165.

19. General Bols, the Chief Administrator of Palestine, asserted: "They [the Zionist Commission] seek, not justice from the military occupant, but that in every question in which a Jew is interested discrimination in his favor shall be shown." Quoted in Barbour, *op. cit.*, p. 109.

20 Graves, *op. cit.*, p. 167.

21 *Trial and Error*, p. 275.

22 Jeffries, *op. cit.*, p. 371.

23 The fact that the Zionists did fail to face the Arab problem is borne out by the self-contradictory attitude of Weizmann toward the Arabs. In one breath he would defiantly announce to the Arabs that the Zionists were migrating to Palestine as of right, or that the settlement work of the Jews was the road that led to Jewish statehood. In the other, he would deny that Zionists even entertained the idea of building Palestine at the expense of others. See Weisgal, *op. cit.*, pp. 55-56, 59.

24 Andrews, *op. cit.*, I, 314.

25 Jeffries, *op. cit.*, p. 42.

26 Moshe Perlmann, "Chapters of Arab-Jewish Diplomacy, 1918-1922," *Jewish Social Studies*, VI (April, 1944), 124.

27 *Ibid.*

28 See above, p. 7.

29 Antonius, *op. cit.*, p. 259.

30 Graves, *op. cit.,* p. 251.

31 John De Vere Loder, *The Truth about Mesopotamia, Palestine and Syria* (London: George Allen & Unwin, Ltd., 1923), pp. 125-126.

32 The Sherif of Mecca, Hussein al-Hashimi, was the titular leader of the Arab Revolt in World War I.

33 Antonius, *op. cit.,* p. 268.

34 Perlmann, *op. cit.,* p. 130.

35 Emir Feisal was the son of the Sherif of Mecca and the military leader of the Arab Revolt.

36 See text in Antonius, *op. cit.,* pp. 437-439.

37 See text in Antonius, *op. cit.,* pp. 433-436.

38 Perlmann, *op. cit.,* pp. 139-141.

39 *Ibid.,* p. 133.

40 Temperley, *op. cit.,* VI, 177.

41 *Ibid.*

42 Toynbee, *op. cit.,* VIII, 306.

43 See text in Hurewitz, *op. cit.,* II, 104.

44 Even Lord Grey, who had supported Zionism when he was Foreign Secretary, asserted in 1923 that the Balfour Declaration was self-contradictory and implied a threat to Arab interests. See Barbour, *op. cit.,* pp. 122-123.

45 Toynbee, *op. cit.,* VIII, 306.

46 *Trial and Error,* p. 280.

47 The ESCO Foundation, *op. cit.,* I, 176.

48 *Trial and Error,* p. 284.

49 *Ibid.,* pp. 284, 287.

50 *Ibid.,* p. 289.

51 The ESCO Foundation, *op. cit.,* I, 176.

52 *Trial and Error,* p. 289.

53 *Ibid.*

54 See "The Zionist Organization's Memorandum to the Supreme Council at the Peace Conference," in Hurewitz, *op. cit.,* II, 45-50.

55 *Trial and Error,* p. 290.

56 The ESCO Foundation, *op. cit.,* I, 270-272.

57 *Trial and Error,* pp. 289-290.

58 *Ibid.,* p. 290.

59 See text in Hurewitz, *op. cit.,* II, 103-106.

60 *Trial and Error,* pp. 290-291.

61 The ESCO Foundation, *op. cit.,* I, 287.

62 See text in Hurewitz, *op. cit.,* II, 106-111.

63 *Trial and Error,* p. 294.

64 Weisgal, *op. cit.,* p. 57.

65 *Trial and Error,* p. 280.

NOTES—CHAPTER IV

1 Israel Cohen, *The Zionist Movement* (London: Frederick Muller, Ltd., 1945), pp. 123-125. Zionist Conferences should be differentiated from the Congresses. They were convened in years when no Congress was assembled.

2 Cohen, *A Short History of Zionism*, p. 85.

3 Cohen, *The Zionist Movement*, p. 125.

4 *Ibid.*, pp. 125-126.

5 *Ibid.*, p. 126.

6 *Ibid.*, pp. 127-132.

7 Cohen, *A Short History of Zionism*, p. 48.

8 Cohen, *The Zionist Movement*, p. 131.

9 Antonius, *op. cit.*, pp. 388-389. The Arabs had no such voice with the Permanent Mandates Commission in Geneva.

10 The Jewish community in Palestine was represented by a Constituent Assembly (Asefath Hanivharim) which elected a National Council (Vaad Leumi). A Rabbinical Council was also established.

11 *Trial and Error*, p. 295.

12 Hurewitz, *op. cit.*, II, 107-108.

13 Cohen, *The Zionist Movement*, p. 170.

14 *Trial and Error*, pp. 305-306.

15 Cohen, *A Short History of Zionism*, p. 124.

16 *Trial and Error*, p. 306; Cohen, *A Short History of Zionism*, pp. 87-88.

17 *Trial and Error*, p. 307.

18 Cohen, *The Zionist Movement*, p. 170.

19 Cohen, *A Short History of Zionism*, p. 125.

20 *Ibid.*

21 Frederick H. Kisch, *Palestine Diary* (London: Victor Gollancz, Ltd., 1938), p. 238.

22 *Trial and Error*, p. 307.

23 *Ibid.*, pp. 308-309.

24 *Ibid.*, pp. 309-311.

25 *Ibid.*, p. 310.

26 Cohen, *A Short History of Zionism*, p. 125.

27 *Ibid.*, pp. 126-127.

28 *Trial and Error*, p. 314.

29 Cohen, *A Short History of Zionism*, p. 127. Also, the membership of the Agency was to be selected by the Z. O. See Parkes, *op. cit.*, p. 307.

30 *Trial and Error*, pp. 313-314.

NOTES—CHAPTER V

1 The ESCO Foundation, *op. cit.*, I, 288.

2 *Trial and Error*, p. 326.

3 *Ibid.*

4 Cohen, *A Short History of Zionism*, p. 254.

5 The ESCO Foundation, *op. cit.*, I. 318.

6 *Ibid.*, I, 317.

7 *Ibid.*, I, 316.

8 Andrews, *op. cit.*, II, 26.

9 *Trial and Error*, p. 300.

10 *Ibid.*, p. 301.

11 The ESCO Foundation, *op. cit.*, II, 624.

12 *Ibid.*, II, 625.

13 *Trial and Error,* p. 332.
14 Cohen, *A Short History of Zionism,* p. 131.
15 The ESCO Foundation, *op. cit.,* II, 645.
16 *Ibid.,* II, 648.
17 *Trial and Error,* p. 333.
18 *Ibid.;* also, Cohen, *A Short History of Zionism,* p. 132.
19 *Trial and Error,* p. 334.
20 *Ibid.*
21 *Ibid.*
22 Barnet Litvinoff, *Ben-Gurion of Israel* (London: Weidenfeld & Nicolson, 1954), p. 102.
23 Cohen, *A Short History of Zionism, p. 132.*
24 *Trial and Error,* p. 335.
25 *Ibid.*
26 Cohen, *A Short History of Zionism,* p. 255.
27 Parkes, *op. cit.,* p. 322.
28 *Ibid.*
29 The ESCO Foundation, *op. cit.,* II, 783.
30 Parkes, *op. cit.,* p. 323.
31 *Ibid.*
32 The ESCO Foundation, *op. cit.,* II, 820.
33 *Ibid.,* II, 859-860.
34 George Lenczowski, *The Middle East in World Affairs* (Ithaca, N. Y.: Cornell University Press, 1953), p. 270.
35 *Trial and Error,* p. 386.
36 Parkes, *op. cit.,* pp. 328-330.
37 Lenczowski, *op. cit.,* p. 269.
38 *Ibid.,* pp. 271-272.

NOTES—CHAPTER VI

1 Kirk, *op. cit.,* p. 13.
2 The ESCO Foundation, *op. cit.,* II, 1080. The revised position was first formulated, according to this source, by the Palestine Zionist Executive in Jerusalem.
3 Kirk, *op. cit.,* p. 232.
4 *Ibid.*
5 *Trial and Error,* pp. 418-419.
6 The ESCO Foundation, *op. cit.,* II, 1079-1080.
7 Chaim Weizmann, "Palestine's Role in the Solution of the Jewish Problem," *Foreign Affairs,* January, 1942, pp. 324-338.
8 Kirk, *op. cit.,* p. 234.
9 *Ibid.,* p. 307.
10 *Ibid.,* p. 233.
11 *Ibid.*
12 *Ibid.,* p. 242.
13 *Ibid.* On page 243, Kirk also notes that Nahum Goldmann went a step further by defining the territory of Jewish national interest as including Transjordan.

14 *Ibid.*, p. 243, footnote.

15 Hurewitz, *op. cit.*, II, 234; George E. Kirk, *A Short History of the Middle East* (London: Methuen, 1952), p. 204. The Emergency Committee was formed in America to serve as the wartime headquarters of the Zionist Organization.

16 The ESCO Foundation, *op. cit.*, II, 1080-1083.

17 It should be noted here that on the eve of the war, the Agency was converted into a Zionist body; see Jacob C. Hurewitz, *The Struggle for Palestine* (New York: W. W. Norton & Co., 1950), p. 157.

18 The ESCO Foundation, *op. cit.*, II, 1082.

19 *Ibid.*, II, 1083.

20 See text in Hurewitz, *Diplomacy in the Near and Middle East*, II, 234-235.

21 This assertion was made in spite of the fact that the Churchill White Paper of 1922 denied that the purpose of the Balfour Declaration was to make Palestine "as Jewish as England is English" or that the development of the Jewish National Home meant the imposition of Jewish nationality upon the inhabitants of Palestine as a whole.

22 The ESCO Foundation, *op. cit.*, II, 1087.

23 This refers to the Inner General Council. See below, p. 64.

24 *Ibid.*

25 See Kermit Roosevelt, "The Partition of Palestine: a Lesson in Pressure Politics," *Middle East Journal*, January, 1948, p. 4: The Biltmore Program had been endorsed by the General Council in 1942 in spite of opposition among Jews in the United States and Palestine.

26 See text of Resolutions of the World Zionist Conference, August, 1945, in *Documents Relating to the Palestine Problem* (London: The Jewish Agency for Palestine, 1945), pp. 94-96. These resolutions were endorsed by the twenty-second Zionist Congress in December, 1946.

27 Roosevelt, *op. cit.*, p. 3.

28 *Ibid.*, p. 4.

29 Lenczowski, *op. cit.*, p. 274.

30 The ESCO Foundation, *op. cit.*, II, 1078.

31 *Ibid.*, II, 1079. The Council also contained members of the leftist labor group and the State Party (an extremist group which insisted openly on the establishment of the Jewish State in Transjordan as well as Palestine).

32 *Ibid.*

33 Hurewitz, *The Struggle for Palestine*, p. 158.

34 The ESCO Foundation, *op. cit.*, II, 1078.

35 Hurewitz, *The Struggle for Palestine*, p. 158.

36 Hurewitz, *Diplomacy in the Near and Middle East*, II, 234. Apparently, the Inner General Council, which may be simply another name for the London or Palestine Executives, was the wartime policy-making headquarters of Zionism, while the Emergency Council was the operational headquarters.

NOTES—CHAPTER VII

1 Hurewitz, *The Struggle for Palestine*, p. 142.

2 *Trial and Error*, p. 418.

3 See above, pp. 12-18.

4 See above, pp. 56-57.

5 Hurewitz, *The Struggle for Palestine*, p. 142.

6 See The ESCO Foundation, *op. cit.*, II, 945-947.

7 Hurewitz, *The Struggle for Palestine*, p. 142.

8 Kirk, *The Middle East in the War*, pp. 240-241.

9 *Trial and Error*, p. 403.

10 Hurewitz, *The Struggle for Palestine*, p. 143.

11 *Trial and Error*, p. 436.

12 Hurewitz, *The Struggle for Palestine*, pp. 144, 215.

13 *Ibid.*, p. 208.

14 *Ibid.*, p. 144.

15 *Ibid.*, p. 208.

16 *Ibid.*

17 Lenczowski, *op. cit.*, p. 272.

18 Cohen, *A Short History of Zionism*, pp. 156-157.

19 Kirk, *The Middle East in the War*, p. 231. The division was to have a flag of its own.

20 *Trial and Error*, p. 424.

21 *Ibid.*, pp. 424-425.

22 *Ibid.*, p. 424.

23 *New Judaea*, XVI (September, 1940) , 192.

24 The ESCO Foundation, *op. cit.*, II, 1029-1032.

25 *Ibid.*, II, 1032.

26 Kirk, *The Middle East in the War*, p. 321. The Brigade's creation was regarded by the Zionists as a proclamation of Israel.

27 The ESCO Foundation, *op. cit.*, II, 1034.

28 Arthur Koestler, *Promise and Fulfillment, Palestine, 1917-1949* (New York: Macmillan, 1949) , pp. 83-84. On p. 335 Koestler states that he has long been a Zionist supporter.

29 Hurewitz, *The Struggle for Palestine*, pp. 204-205.

30 *Trial and Error*, p. 436.

31 *Ibid.*

32 Kirk, *The Middle East in the War*, pp. 13-14, 234; also, Kirk, *A Short History of the Middle East*, p. 210.

33 Hurewitz, *The Struggle for Palestine*, p. 196.

34 Kirk, *The Middle East in the War*, p. 229.

35 Hurewitz, *The Struggle for Palestine*, p. 196.

36 For a full description of this organization, see Jon and David Kimche, *The Secret Roads, the "Illegal Migration of a People," 1938-1948* (London: Secker and Warburg, 1955) .

37 See The ESCO Foundation, *op. cit.*, II, 942-955.

38 *Ibid.*, II, 946.

39 *Trial and Error*, p. 304.

40 Kirk, *The Middle East in the War*, pp. 13-14.

41 *Ibid.*, pp. 307-308.

42 The ESCO Foundation, *op. cit.*, II, 1036.

43 Kirk, *The Middle East in the War*, p. 310.

44 Koestler, *op. cit.*, p. 12.

1 Hurewitz, *The Struggle for Palestine*, p. 144.
2 Roosevelt, *op. cit.*, p. 4.
3 Hurewitz, *The Struggle for Palestine*, pp. 209-210. This was in addition to its role in relation to the World Zionist Movement.
4 *Ibid.*, p. 210.
5 *Ibid.*, p. 144. The American Palestine Committee's initial membership included 67 Senators, 143 members of the House, and 22 governors.
6 *Ibid.*, p. 210.
7 Kirk, *The Middle East in the War*, p. 330.
8 Hurewitz, *The Struggle for Palestine*, p. 210.
9 Elmer Berger, *The Jewish Dilemma* (New York: The Devin-Adair Co., 1946) , p. 163.
10 *Ibid.*, p. 165.
11 *Ibid.*, p. 166.
12 Hurewitz, *The Struggle for Palestine*, p. 210.
13 Berger, *op. cit.*, pp. 165-166.
14 Alfred M. Lilienthal, *What Price Israel* (Chicago: Henry Regnery Co., 1953) , p. 18.
15 *Ibid.*
16 Kirk, *The Middle East in the War*, p. 329, footnote.
17 Berger, *op. cit.*, p. 165.
18 See below, pp. 92-93.
19 Hurewitz, *The Struggle for Palestine*, p. 211.
20 The ESCO Foundation, *op. cit.*, II, 1088-1089.
21 *Ibid.*, II, 1091.
22 *Ibid.*, II, 1093-1094.
23 The original principle of the Jewish Agency was the cooperation of Zionist and non-Zionist Jews in the work of assisting the Jewish community in Palestine. It was bi-partisan in original intention.
24 Kirk, *The Middle East in the War*, p. 247.
25 Frank Charles Sakran, *Palestine Dilemma, Arab Rights versus Zionist Aspirations* (Washington, D. C.: Public Affairs Press, 1948) , p. 168.
26 Hurewitz, *The Struggle for Palestine*, p. 213.
27 The ESCO Foundation, *op. cit.*, II, 1115.
28 Lenczowski, *op. cit.*, p. 274.
29 Sakran, *op. cit.*, p. 169.
30 *Ibid.*
31 *Ibid.*, p. 170.
32 *Ibid.*
33 *Ibid.*, pp. 171-172.
34 *Ibid.*, pp. 172-173.
35 Roosevelt, *op. cit.*, p. 4.
36 *Trial and Error*, p. 420.
37 *Ibid.*, p. 425.
38 *Ibid.*
39 *Ibid.*, p. 431.
40 *Ibid.*, p. 435.

41 See above, pp. 33-34.
42 Kirk, *The Middle East in the War*, p. 314.
43 See text in The ESCO Foundation, *op. cit.*, II, 1116.
44 Kirk, *The Middle East in the War*, p. 328.
45 Roosevelt, *op. cit.*, p. 5.

NOTES—CHAPTER IX

1 Kirk, *The Middle East in the War*, p. 327.
2 *Memoirs by Harry S. Truman* (Garden City, N.Y.: Doubleday & Co., Inc., 1956), II *(Years of Trial and Hope)*, 132-133. Copyright held by Time, Inc.
3 *Ibid.*
4 *Ibid.*, II, 133.
5 David E. Hirsch, *A Record of American Zionism* (New York: Zionist Organization of America, 1956), p. 23. In July, 1945, Truman was urged to support Zionist aspirations through correspondence signed by nearly 300 members of Congress and 40 governors.
6 *Memoirs by Harry S. Truman*, II, 138-139.
7 Sakran, *op. cit.*, p. 175.
8 *Memoirs by Harry S. Truman*, II, 133.
9 *Ibid.*, II, 139-141.
10 Roosevelt, *op. cit.*, p. 11.
11 Sakran, *op. cit.*, p. 181.
12 *Memoirs by Harry S. Truman*, II, 140.
13 *Ibid.*, II, 143-144.
14 *Ibid.*, II, 144-145.
15 See above, p. 49.
16 Morris L. Ernst, *So Far So Good* (New York: Harper and Brothers, 1948), pp. 176-177.
17 Toynbee, *op. cit.*, VIII, 307.
18 Lilienthal, *op. cit.*, p. 34.
19 Roosevelt, *op. cit.*, p. 12.
20 Walter Millis and E. S. Duffield (eds.), *The Forrestal Diaries* (New York: Viking Press, 1951), p. 304. In 1947, Truman told his Cabinet that he would make no statement on Palestine. He said he had stuck his neck out once (1945) and would not do it again.
21 *Ibid.*, pp. 188-189.
22 *Trial and Error*, p. 440.
23 *Ibid.*
24 *Ibid.*
25 See above, pp. 83-87.
26 Hurewitz, *The Struggle for Palestine*, pp. 253-255.
27 Sakran, *op. cit.*, p. 182, footnote.
28 *Forrestal Diaries*, p. 180.
29 See Bartley C. Crum, *Behind the Silken Curtain, a Personal Account of Anglo-American Diplomacy in Palestine and the Middle East* (New York: Simon & Schuster, 1947).

30 The Zionists tried to offset the disadvantages for them in the Report by publicizing those recommendations favorable to Zionism and presenting them as the whole Report. Kirk, *Short History of the Middle East,* p. 213.

31 See summary of the Committee's report in The ESCO Foundation, *op. cit.,* II, 1221-1234.

32 Hurewitz, *The Struggle for Palestine,* pp. 257-262.

33 Sakran, *op. cit.,* p. 186.

34 *Ibid.*

35 *Ibid.,* p. 187.

36 Hurewitz, *The Struggle for Palestine,* p. 237.

37 Abcarius, *op. cit.,* p. 223.

38 *Palestine, Statement of Information relating to Acts of Violence* (Cmd. 6873, July 1946), p. 4. The Stern Group was an extremist offshoot of the Irgun Zvai Leumi.

39 Kirk, *A Short History of the Middle East,* p. 210.

40 Sakran, *op. cit.,* p. 161.

41 Kirk, *A Short History of the Middle East,* p. 210.

42 Hurewitz, *The Struggle for Palestine,* pp. 238-239.

43 Kirk, *A Short History of the Middle East,* p. 215.

44 Lenczowski, *op. cit.,* pp. 276-277, footnote.

45 Kirk, *A Short History of the Middle East,* p. 215.

46 *Ibid.,* p. 216.

47 *Ibid.* This systematic Zionist selection of immigrants as it operated before the Second World War is described in Abraham Revusky, *Jews in Palestine* (New York: Bloch Publishing Co., 1945), pp. 220-221.

48 Lenczowski, *op. cit.,* pp. 276-277, footnote. It is significant that this underground, which is now acknowledged and described in detail in Jon and David Kimche's *The Secret Roads,* was considered something to hide by Lehman.

49 Kirk, *A Short History of the Middle East,* p. 216.

50 The account given in *The Secret Roads* leaves no doubt as to the certainty of this statement.

51 Sakran, *op. cit.,* p. 189.

52 *Ibid.,* pp. 190-192.

53 *Memoirs by Harry S. Truman,* II, 155.

54 *Trial and Error,* p. 458.

55 *Ibid.,* p. 459.

56 Roosevelt, *op. cit.,* p. 14.

57 *Ibid.,* pp. 14-15.

58 *Forrestal Diaries,* p. 346.

59 *Ibid.*

60 *Ibid.,* pp. 357-358.

61 *Ibid.,* p. 346.

62 *Ibid.,* p. 358.

63. Roosevelt, *op. cit.,* p. 14.

64 *Memoirs by Harry S. Truman,* II, 158.

65 *Ibid.*

66 *Ibid.*

67 *Ibid.,* II, 160.

68 *Ibid.*, II, 160-161.

69 In spite of its irrelevancies and implications, the line of reasoning behind this appeal was never questioned by the President.

70 *Memoirs by Harry S. Truman*, II, 164.

71 *Forrestal Diaries*, p. 441.

NOTES FOR EPILOGUE

1 See The ESCO Foundation, *op. cit.*, I, 93.

2 Actually, less than twenty percent of world Jewry live in Israel. Not one percent of American Jewry has emigrated to Israel.

3 Hurewitz, *Diplomacy in the Near and Middle East*, II, 48.

4 *Trial and Error*, p. 290.

5 *Ibid.*, p. 289.

6 State of Israel, *Government Yearbook*, 5713 (1952), p. 15.

7 *Ibid.*, 5716 (1955), p. 320. This quote from Ben Gurion is followed by two paradoxical assertions, one to the effect that the historical frontiers of Eretz Israel are fixed and given to the Jews since the beginning of time, and the other insisting that the State of Israel will honor its present boundaries. It is difficult to ascertain Ben Gurion's true feelings on this matter.

8 State of Israel, *Facts and Figures*, 1955, pp. 18-20.

9 David Ben Gurion, *Israel, the Tasks Ahead* (New York: Israel Office of Information, 1949), p. 4: "The establishment of the State of Israel was merely the first stage in the fulfillment of our historic vision. . . . The ingathering of our exiles is the prerequisite to the realization of this great dream in its full human implications." See also, *David Ben Gurion Selections* (New York: Zionist Labor Organization of America, 1948), p. 75: "The promotion of Jewish immigration is not only the central task of the Jewish State—but the essential justification for its establishment and existence."

10 *The Jerusalem Post*, July 23, 1951, p. 1.

11 Karl Baum, "Zionism, Diaspora and Israel," *Zionist Review*, July 13, 1951, p. 10.

12 *The Jerusalem Post*, August 17, 1951, p. 5.

13 *Ibid.*

14 State of Israel, *Facts and Figures*, 1955, pp. 17-19.

15 As recently as the summer of 1957, Ben Gurion reasserted: "A Zionist must come to Israel himself as an immigrant." See *Time*, August 26, 1957, p. 55.

16 *The Jerusalem Post*, July 23, 1951, p. 1.

BIBLIOGRAPHY

PRIMARY SOURCES

Ben Gurion, David. *Israel, the Tasks Ahead.* New York: Israel Office of Information, 1949.

Crum, Bartley C. *Behind the Silken Curtain, a Personal Account of Anglo-American Diplomacy in Palestine and the Middle East.* New York: Simon & Schuster, 1947.

David Ben Gurion Selections. New York: Zionist Labor Organization of America, 1948.

Documents Relating to the Palestine Problem. London: The Jewish Agency for Palestine, 1945.

Ernst, Morris L. *So Far So Good.* New York: Harper and Brothers, 1948.

Goldmann, Nahum. *The Genius of Herzl and Zionism Today.* Jerusalem: Zionist Executive, 1955.

Herzl, Theodor. *The Jewish State, an Attempt at a Modern Solution of the Jewish Question.* Translated by Sylvie D'Avigdor. New York: Scopus Publishing Co., 1943.

Hurewitz, Jacob C. *Diplomacy in the Near and Middle East, a Documentary Record,* 2 vols. Princeton, N.J.: D. Van Nostrand Co., Inc., 1956.

Kisch, Frederick H. *Palestine Diary.* London: Victor Gollancz, Ltd., 1938.

Memoirs by Harry S. Truman. Vol. II *(Years of Trial and Hope).* Garden City, N. Y.: Doubleday & Co., Inc., 1956.

Millis, Walter and Duffield, E. S. (editors). *The Forrestal Diaries.* New York: Viking Press, 1951.

Palestine, Statement of Information relating to Acts of Violence (Cmd. 6873, July 1946).

State of Israel. *Facts and Figures,* 1955.

State of Israel. *Government Yearbook,* 5713 (1952), 5716 (1955), 5718 (1957).

Stearns, Raymond P. *Pageant of Europe: Sources and Selections from the Renaissance to the Present Day.* New York: Harcourt, Brace & Co., Inc., 1947.

Temperley, Harold W. V. (editor). *A History of the Peace Conference of Paris,* Vol. VI. London: Henry Frowde & Hodder & Stoughton, 1924.

Trial and Error, the Autobiography of Chaim Weizmann. New York: Harper and Brothers, 1949.

SECONDARY SOURCES

Books

Abcarius, M. F. *Palestine through the Fog of Propaganda.* London: Hutchinson & Co., N. D.

Andrews, Fannie Fern. *The Holy Land under Mandate.* 2 vols. Cambridge, Mass.: Houghton Mifflin Co., 1931.

Antonius, George. *The Arab Awakening, the Story of the Arab National Movement.* London: Hamish Hamilton, 1945.

Barbour, Nevill. *Palestine: Star or Crescent.* New York: Odyssey Press, 1947.

Berger, Elmer. *The Jewish Dilemma.* New York: The Devin-Adair Co., 1945.

Cohen, Israel. *A Short History of Zionism.* London: Frederick Muller, Ltd., 1951.

———— *The Zionist Movement.* London: Frederick Muller, Ltd., 1945.

The ESCO Foundation for Palestine, Inc. *Palestine, a Study of Jewish, Arab, and British Policies.* 2 vols. New Haven: Yale University Press, 1947.

Graves, Philip. *Palestine, the Land of Three Faiths.* London: Jonathan Cape, 1923.

Hirsch, David E. *A Record of American Zionism*. New York: Zionist Organization of America, 1956.

Hurewitz, Jacob C., *The Struggle for Palestine*. New York: W. W. Norton & Co., 1950.

Jastrow, Morris, Jr. *Zionism and the Future of Palestine, the Fallacies and Dangers of Political Zionism*. New York: The Macmillan Company, 1919.

Jeffries, Joseph M. N. *Palestine: the Reality*. London: Longmans, Green & Co., 1939.

Kimche, Jon and David. *The Secret Roads, the "Illegal Migration of a People," 1938-1948*. London: Sacker and Warburg, 1955.

Kirk, George E. *The Middle East in the War*. London: Oxford University Press, 1953.

———— *A Short History of the Middle East from the Rise of Islam to Modern Times*. London: Methuen, 1952.

Koestler, Arthur. *Promise and Fulfillment, Palestine, 1917-1949*. New York: The Macmillan Company, 1949.

Lenczowski, George. *The Middle East in World Affairs*. Ithaca, New York: Cornell University Press, 1953.

Lilienthal, Alfred M. *What Price Israel*. Chicago: Henry Regnery Co., 1953.

Litvinoff, Barnet. *Ben Gurion of Israel*. London: Weidenfeld & Nicolson, 1954.

Loder, John De Vere. *The Truth About Mesopotamia, Palestine and Syria*. London: George Allen & Unwin, Ltd., 1923.

Newbigin, Bishop Lesslie. *The Household of God*. New York: Friendship Press, 1954.

Parkes, James William. *A History of Palestine from 135 A.D. to Modern Times*. London: Victor Gollancz, Ltd., 1949.

Pieters, Albertus. *The Seed of Abraham, a Biblical Study of Israel, the Church, and the Jew*. Grand Rapids, Michigan: Eerdmans Publishing Co., 1950.

Revusky, Abraham, *Jews in Palestine*. New York: Bloch Publishing Co., 1945.

Sakran, Frank Charles. *Palestine Dilemma, Arab Rights versus*

Zionist Aspirations. Washington, D. C.: Public Affairs Press, 1948.

Sokolow, Nahum, *History of Zionism 1600-1918.* Vol. I. London: Longmans, Green & Co., 1919.

Sykes, Christopher. *Two Studies in Virtue.* New York: Alfred A. Knopf, 1953.

Toynbee, Arnold J. *A Study of History.* Vol. VIII. London: Oxford University Press, 1954.

Weisgal, Meyer W. (editor). *Chaim Weizmann, Statesman, Scientist and Builder of the Jewish Commonwealth.* New York: Dial Press, 1944.

Periodicals

Baum, Karl. "Zionism, Diaspora and Israel," *Zionist Review,* July 13, 1951.

The Jerusalem Post, July 23, 1951, August 17, 1951.

New Judaea, XVI (September, 1940).

Perlmann, Moshe. *"Chapters of Arab-Jewish Diplomacy, 1918-1922,"* Jewish Social Studies, VI (April, 1944).

Roosevelt, Kermit. "The Partition of Palestine: a Lesson in Pressure Politics," *Middle East Journal,* January, 1948.

Time, August 26, 1957.

Weizmann, Chaim. *"Palestine's Role in the Solution of the* Jewish Problem," *Foreign Affairs,* January, 1942.

INDEX

132